SOCIOMETRY
IN GROUP RELATIONS

Sociometry
in Group Relations

A MANUAL FOR TEACHERS

HELEN HALL JENNINGS

SECOND EDITION

GREENWOOD PRESS, PUBLISHERS
WESTPORT, CONNECTICUT

The Library of Congress has catalogued this publication as follows:

Library of Congress Cataloging in Publication Data

Jennings, Helen Hall, 1905-
   Sociometry in group relations.

   Bibliography: p.
   1. Sociometry. 2. Personnel service in education.
I. Title.
[HM253.J4 1973]   301.18'028   72-9829
ISBN 0-8371-6483-4

This edition originally published in 1959 by American Council on Education.

Reprinted with the permission of the American Council on Education.

Reprinted by Greenwood Press, Inc.

First Greenwood reprinting 1973
Second Greenwood reprinting 1977

Library of Congress catalog card number 72-9829

ISBN 0-8371-6483-4

Printed in the United States of America

FOREWORD

THE FIRST EDITION OF *Sociometry in Group Relations* WAS PUB-
lished ten years ago as one of the volumes of the Work in Progress
Series developed by the Intergroup Education in Cooperating
Schools project, which operated from January 1945 through
August 1948 under a committee appointed by the American Council on Education with funds granted by the National Conference
of Christians and Jews. This project was a joint undertaking of
the project staff and teachers and administrators in cooperating
schools and school systems. It sought to develop new approaches,
new techniques, new materials, and new ways of mobilizing school
and community resources for improving human relations and
fostering intergroup understanding. The project produced a number of books reporting experimentation and techniques useful in
working for the improvement of human relations.

Sociometry in Group Relations was developed as a work guide
for elementary and secondary school teachers. The widespread
use of the original edition in the ten years since its publication
indicated the desirability of a revision. Since the staff of the Intergroup Education project had ceased its work, the principal author
of the first edition was engaged to assume full responsibility for
this revision. The author had the assistance of the staff of the Commission on Educational Organizations of the National Conference
of Christians and Jews.

This revised edition is offered as an improved tool to help
teachers understand the children in their classrooms and hence
to improve intergroup relationships for the betterment of child
and of society.

ARTHUR S. ADAMS, *President*
American Council on Education

January 1959

PREFACE TO SECOND EDITION

THE PRESENT PUBLICATION IS NOT ONLY A THOROUGH REVISION OF the earlier edition but also an expansion with a view to enhancing careful, focused sociometric work in the classroom. The major findings of research since 1948, which throw light on the meaning of sociometric structure and sociometric choice, among school children particularly, are reported and discussed. These findings indicate that it is appropriate and central to the educative process that the teacher take more than a passing interest in sociometric method. They show that the way an individual feels about himself depends to a large extent upon the way others feel about him and he toward others. The kind of use an individual may or can make of being literate or capable in other learnings may depend on his self-esteem. Indeed, the view of himself he has developed in the course of growing up may affect the direction and the quality of his future mental and emotional growth and to what purposes he is able to put any of his learnings.

The school as an institution is limited in what it can do to modify the home's influence on how the individual views himself. But at least within the school setting the systematic use of sociometric procedures enables the faculty to cultivate the role of social relationships for a more fortunate development of everyone. This is made possible because sociometric method tends to widen the faculty's awareness of the needs of all pupils and, thus, to prevent exclusive attention to those who have marked emotional difficulties.

As educators notice the differing developmental effects of the individual's ability to make contacts which will aid him to mature, or his inability to do so, or his lack of ability to see hardly at all beyond himself, it appears certain they will not leave to chance opportunities to provide for the individual's gaining a feeling of

vii

well-being about himself and in relation to others. Sociometric research, to which the contribution of teachers has been paramount, offers fundamental help in this direction.

Many aspects of the intercultural validity of sociometric findings and interpretations presented in this publication are borne out by the work of Paul Maucorps with child and adult populations in France, of Ake Bjerstedt with children in Sweden, and of Albert Husquinet with boys in Belgium. Work in West Germany, Japan, and Turkey give further confirmation. Of especial importance in this connection is some twenty-five years of Canadian research, under the leadership of Mary L. Northway, which offers new and basic knowledge of childhood, from the earliest years on.

The author wishes to acknowledge her appreciation for permission to use the following: to Harper and Brothers, for materials from her chapter "Sociometric Structure in Personality and Group Formation," in *Group Relations at the Crossroads* edited by Muzafer Sherif and M. O. Wilson; to the Association for Supervision and Curriculum Development of the National Education Association for the sociograms appearing on pages 68–69, 94, and 95 of the present book and for excerpts from her chapter in *Fostering Mental Health in Our Schools* edited by Caroline Tryon.

The author thanks Helen E. Davis for editing the manuscript.

HELEN HALL JENNINGS

Brooklyn College

January 1959

CONTENTS

FOREWORD *by Arthur S. Adams*............................. v

PREFACE TO SECOND EDITION........................... vii

LIST OF FIGURES.. xi

I. GROUP RELATIONS AND EDUCATION................. 1
Evidences of Growing Bewilderment 1
The Importance of Group Relations 3

II. THE SOCIOMETRIC TEST 11
The Distinctiveness of Sociograms 12
Administering the Sociometric Test 13
Making the Sociogram 20
Following Up the Clues 26
Successive Sociograms and Time Intervals 44

III. USES AND APPLICATIONS............................ 48
Carrying Out the Original Agreement 48
Assisting Individual Children 52
Reshaping General Practices 55
Grouping for Work 58
Grouping for Clubs 60
Analyzing Cleavages 66

IV. SOCIOMETRIC FINDINGS SUMMARIZED................ 71
The Nature of Children's Choices 72
Characteristic Emphases by Age Level 74
Factors in the Classroom Atmosphere 78
Some Characteristics of Association Patterns 81
Summary 86

V. PSYCHOLOGICAL THEORY OF SOCIOMETRIC CHOICES ... 88

    The Psychological Staircase Phenomenon 88

    *The Psychological Staircase and Discrimination in Making
       Choices* 90

    Psychegroup and Sociogroup Continuum 91

    The Necessity for Psychegroup Satisfaction 96

    Assessment of Choice and Group Structure 98

BIBLIOGRAPHY 100

INDEX 103

LIST OF FIGURES

1. *Sociometric Tabulation Form* 21
2. *Tally of Sociometric Positions* 23
3. *A Filled-In Sociogram Form, Presenting Graphically the Choice Patterns* 25
4. *Girl Scout Sociogram* 68–69
5. *Sociogram of a First-Grade Class, Showing Usual Trends of Interpersonal Structure* 76
6. *Sociogram of a Sixth-Grade Class, Showing Usual Trends of Interpersonal Structure* 77
7. *Sociogram of a First-Grade Class, Showing Interpersonal Structure under an Atmosphere Promoting Interaction* .. 82
8. *Sociogram of a Sixth-Grade Class, Showing Interpersonal Structure under an Atmosphere Promoting Interaction* .. 83
9. *Sociogram of a Fifth-Grade Class, Showing Interpersonal Structure under an Atmosphere Restricting Interaction* .. 85
10. *Sociogram of an Eighth-Grade Class, Showing Psyche-group Interaction* 94
11. *Sociogram of an Eighth-Grade Class, Showing Sociogroup Motivation* 95

I. GROUP RELATIONS AND EDUCATION

WHENEVER HUMAN BEINGS COME TOGETHER, THEY FORM LINES OF association and set up the process of social interaction. The quality of these associations produces what is called an atmosphere for the group. This is true in classrooms as well as in other social settings. In this social interaction the roles which individuals play are determined. Some individuals come to the fore in the esteem of their classmates, while the efforts of others to join in are resisted. In this atmosphere, furthermore, some individuals are secure and happy, while others may be rejected or frustrated in their social participation.

All learning in school takes place within the setting of pupil-pupil relationships. Teachers, in general, realize that the individual's personal and academic growth can be affected adversely or favorably by his position in the group and that all pupils stimulate or thwart each other in many ways. What is not usually so well realized, however, is that the social atmosphere is very largely created and maintained by pupil interaction, and this can be constructively influenced by the tone the teacher sets and the grouping practices she uses. A dominantly decisive factor is the constellation of attraction and rejection linked with the values that operate among the boys and girls themselves. Schools need to know what these interpersonal relations are like, how they function, and how they affect behavior and learning. While various techniques for studying the individual child are available, techniques for assessing group life are much scantier.

EVIDENCES OF GROWING BEWILDERMENT

Perhaps the most important thing to note about children's responses to each other is that they differ significantly both from

1

their response to adults and from adults' responses to them. Some teachers have been surprised to discover, through the sociometric devices to be described in the next chapter, that a quiet, well-mannered, and excellent student may not be at all liked by his classmates. They have been even more surprised, at times, to find that in the same class another, to all appearances, equally gentle and able child is in the highest favor. Furthermore, the so-called problem children often feel particularly attracted to an individual of this kind. The basis for the whole distinction is not immediately apparent and may never be completely understood. But it is clear that the children are developing and using their own means of assessing one another. They are also generating an emotional climate for the class—colored by their own loves and hates and reflecting their loyalties and standards—that may have bearing on their reactions to the teacher's behavior.

The extent to which clues to this underlying network of affectional ties and prestige relations come out into the open in school is, of course, related to the teacher's efforts and degree of rapport with the children. But the absence of overt signs generally means that there is relatively little free give and take between teacher and class, not that interpersonal association is less important. Even in equally permissive atmospheres, some teachers will be quicker than others to notice certain aspects of the children's group life. For instance, Miss X may observe that every time she has dealings with Jack, his reactions are definitely linked to, if not precipitated by, Dan's behavior. This may suggest to her that the cooperation of both pupils may be secured by recognizing their importance to each other. A less perceptive teacher might not have caught on for a period of weeks or might have missed the point entirely.

Usually the situation is more complicated, as in the case of Miss Y's eighth-grade class in a large city. This teacher is ingenious at introducing topics and imaginative projects to her pupils; she gets the discussion going by telling a story, or describing an incident, or asking a provocative question. Frequently, however, the exchange of ideas gets out of hand. Jim and Harry start contradicting each other, the others take sides, more heat than light is generated, and the argument ends nowhere. Or, again, if Bob makes an important point in response to Miss Y's lead, as he often does, Bill and Joe and Tom slump in their seats, sulk, and refuse to say anything. But if Mary should happen to make the very same suggestion, the boys would come to life and back her up with all their hearts. For whatever reason, both in and out of school, the pupils tend to gang up against each other. Miss Y describes them as "stubborn and quarrelsome and sometimes downright mean."

Another example may be provided by Miss Z's class. This teacher accurately notes that the feelings of her pupils for one another have a lot to do with their receptiveness to her instruction. She has observed that some children are particularly close to one another, but not interested in the others. Since she was troubled by this apparent exclusiveness, she seated known friends as far apart as possible because "after all, the important thing is for them to get their schoolwork done." Girls and boys who did not know one another very well were assigned to the same project in the room. Soon Miss Z observed that there was much commotion in the halls between periods—giggling, shoving, gathering in small groups. Restlessness in class often rose to the pitch of squabbling. Each time there was an outright fight, it was difficult to get the group back to facing the lessons for the day. One boy, after being quiet for weeks, suddenly began to fool around, whisper, and tease. When asked about this, he finally admitted, "Well, the other kids will like me better if I am not too good."

Miss Y and Miss Z are puzzled by what they have to report; they would like to understand precisely what is going on. The point to be emphasized here is that children in both rooms are learning a good deal about human relations, regardless of what their teachers may wish them to learn. Not only is Miss Y's Bob getting the notion that "it doesn't matter what I do!" and storing up resentment that may burst out at any time, but also the other boys are learning the habit of ridiculing and abusing some of their classmates as a matter of course. Both teachers recognize that they must understand situations of this sort if they are to guide their pupils to healthier personal and group behavior, and to get the most out of the school curriculum.

THE IMPORTANCE OF GROUP RELATIONS

Integrating patterns of human relations contribute to educational ends in many ways. They help personal development and increase motivation to learn. Group life itself is important, and some direct preparation for it is needed.

Personal development and learning

The kind of group life in which an individual participates contributes to his personal development. Individuals can fully develop only in interaction with their fellows. The happiness and growth of each individual student depend in large measure on his personal security with his classmates. In a group he also learns to face, to analyze, and to assess problems in a social context, and to develop ways of solving them with others. In interaction with others, furthermore, the broadening of his personal universe takes place; he gets to know his fellows, their values, and ways, and so gradually extends his sensitivity in human relations. His personal social maturity is also dependent on interaction with others. Educators have not always realized this. In many schools each child is treated on a strictly individual basis; what he does or does not do is dealt with as his personal responsibility. Tasks are assigned according to this pattern; satisfactions, whether in the form of marks or other recognition, are similarly awarded; and punishments are likewise given as if shortcomings were entirely an individual matter. The child is thus systematically oriented toward standing on his own feet and rising or falling according to personal achievement only. He is not directed toward facing, analyzing, or assessing problems in a social context or developing plans for solving them with others.

This emphasis on independent action has many harmful effects. The more a child succeeds in learning exclusively by and for himself, the greater the loss to him as an individual. Those who are successful learn not only to individualize all achievement and responsibility, but they also learn to cherish exclusiveness in their social relations and to keep others from undermining their position and prestige. In other words, they are learning how to keep group life as sectionized and divided up as possible in order to safeguard their own standing in some part of it. Other less successful children are learning to withdraw and suppress their rebelliousness, to give up trying to exercise their talents, and to acquiesce in a social situation that is largely responsible for their own failures. They may be afraid to enter social doors that are actually open to them and pass up opportunities where their contributions would really be welcome. Both are apt to get distorted views of themselves as individuals and as members of society.

Neither can we overlook the positive role of interpersonal contacts as a psychological necessity. As children mature, their interests in, and affectional relations to, one another broaden parallel to their expanding capacity to get satisfaction from social intercourse. Children need approval from others of their own age possibly more than the approval of their teachers. They need to grow in their ability to appreciate others, to assess themselves through the eyes of others, and to make a place for themselves. They should have opportunities for socialization, for the exchange of ideas, for helping one another, and for exploring one another's personalities. Without such opportunities their perspective will be foreshortened, their skills for contact with others limited, and their initiative in reaching out toward other people inhibited. This development cannot take place naturally when interpersonal contacts are not sanctioned or when natural inclinations and affinities are disregarded in the social arrangements provided.

Teachers often consider it their duty to separate children who show interest in each other because of the assumed interference with their work. Such was Miss Z's assumption in the above illustration. Seating plans, working committees, and other arrangements are often set up without regard to students' inclinations toward each other, or even in direct opposition to them. Good conditions for learning are thereby destroyed or at best neutralized, not to speak of other possible consequences such as the expression of thwarted tendencies in giggling or teasing, as was illustrated in Miss Z's class. Many a disciplinary problem arises from the fact that children are taught to live two lives, one officially and the other under cover, in order to satisfy the social needs forbidden by the school.

The same thing applies to the frustration of children's efforts to help each other. Girls and boys may be willing and able to explain things to one another with a patience and understanding beyond the ability of busy teachers to summon. When this inclination is thwarted, it can be exercised by subterfuge only. Thus, the child is taught that he must disregard appeals for help, that he must not openly contribute to the social needs of himself or his classmates—in other words, that he must strictly mind his "own" business which, however, is unrealistically defined.

Artificial restrictions of this sort will color a child's outlook on everything in school and even life beyond it. Being emotionally fenced in, in this one aspect of his experience, he comes to regard group life and social interaction as reserved for the unimportant parts of living, possibly as unpleasant, and, thus, as to be avoided in connection with work. He has lost the opportunity to learn how satisfying give and take can be or to learn the personal release that can be had from joint action.

Academic learning in school cannot be separated from the social atmosphere in which it takes place. Since children are taught in groups, they are bound to affect each other. Their attitudes toward one another and their personal feelings of security and belonging have a lot to do with the way they use their minds. Cleavages, interference with communication, and other tensions usually absorb energy that could be used for positive achievement. Many experiments in the project testify to the fact that when the emotional shocks due to inadequate or discordant group life are removed and advantage is taken of the existing psychological affinities, there usually result a heightening and release of children's intellectual abilities along with a redirection of their thinking processes. These outcomes are related not only to what happens to individual personalities, but also to the play of group or social motivation on performance. Positive interaction in learning allows members of a group to complement one another's capacities and hence contributes to greater total achievement. Individuals can stimulate one another in place of competing with one another. But, above all, group motivation adds an extra stimulus which cannot be set up in individuals by themselves, especially when they may be emotionally conditioned for rivalry instead of collaboration. A basis is thus created for the natural discipline resulting from wanting to please other members in a group, from wanting to perform adequately in the group endeavor.

Preparation for group living

Most of us live and work most of the time in groups of one sort or another. To do this successfully, it is important to learn what we can get from and give to others. We need to learn how to play different roles, how to extend our skills for living with others, and to enlarge our concepts of the group and of values beyond those of single individuals. We need to experience achievement as a result of joint effort and learn how to relate our own skills and capacities to group concerns, as well as to get satisfaction from shared purposes. We need to discover that pooled abilities supplement and complement one another and enhance the end result. These skills and attitudes do not develop automatically. Mere physical proximity does not necessarily make a psychological group. Experiences to promote such ends need to be planned for.

Children can begin to learn these things at an early age. By the age of six nearly all children are able to plan and discuss intelligently, or to analyze together under guidance what they may be doing to hurt some other child's feelings. Young children can think of ways to help unhappy children or how to make a newcomer feel at home. Gradually all children can learn the adaptability and flexibility needed in their approach to classmates; they can learn how to give and receive criticism, how to pool ideas, and how to assess what each child has to give or what others need to receive from him. All children need to and can learn how to cultivate the social domain around them.

Preparation for significant interaction cannot be left to incidental occasions or extracurricular activities alone, especially when these are regarded as something in addition to academic activities and, therefore, less important. Participation cannot be regarded as a luxury earned as a reward for individual success in academic matters. All activities in school, from committees to improve student government to campaigns for school funds, can be used to extend the individual's range of social skills. Sixth-graders who are expected to manage patrol groups should have opportunity to discuss the functions involved and the problems which are likely to come up while carrying them out. They can learn how to examine the effects of their own behavior on those they are patrolling. These are situations in which functional leadership skills are learned.

In classroom discussions children need, and can learn how to use, each other's contributions, no matter how varied they may be, how to allow for adequate expression, and mainly how to distill from each person's individual experience what is useful for all. Curricular content can be selected to add to intellectual understanding of these processes and of the ways in which they apply elsewhere.

In all groups, and especially in populations as large as a school enrollment, there are cleavages—between people who seem to be different and those who accept the prevailing standard, between individuals whose conceptions of what is right and wrong diverge. In this respect the school is but a replica of the community outside. Today, ability to deal with conflicts and to prevent disagreement on one point from getting in the way of doing something else together is especially needed.

Group life needs to be studied for ways in which cleavages can be eliminated or skills developed for handling these cleavages in order to avoid their tremendous psychological waste. Perhaps this can best be achieved by allowing a cosmopolitan population to accept its own diversity and thus train itself for meeting differences. A frequent policy of schools is to strive for homogeneity by such devices as ability grouping, the separation of ages, or segregation by courses of study. Often boys and girls eat in different parts of the cafeteria, use different playgrounds, or are admitted and dismissed at different times; interaction between the sexes is thus unnaturally restricted.

All such divisions operate to limit association and the opportunity to develop group skills. Attempts to bring about homogeneity of population with respect to cultural origin, socioeconomic position, scholastic ability, or any other factor—insofar as it is achieved—create a very uninstructive classroom. Important educational aspects of the stimulus of significant exchange can thereby be largely maneuvered out of the situation. An artificial hierarchy of values—perhaps not intended but nevertheless detrimental— tends to be created and adversely affects the sociometric structure and the educative process. It then becomes very difficult for teachers and students alike not to attach different degrees of prestige to the several rungs of the ladder. Such divisions can be particularly dangerous, from the standpoint of developing relations, when children from certain sections of the population or ethnic backgrounds are "guided" into a given course without regard to aptitudes or intellectual grasp. More serious, however, is the fact that sectioning makes for a certain consciousness within each subdivision at the expense of the rest. The others tend to be regarded as "not the thing" or perhaps even as "the enemy." Unrealistic and emotionalized mutual assessments are likely to arise and result in misunderstanding. These in turn affect not only the amount and kind of social contact each set may have, but also the way each thinks about itself and about those from whom it is shut off. In this way a number of stereotypes are built up. The ideas each section may have developed tend to become rigid and static or even protective and resistant to the effects of open communication. The loss to individual personality as well as to group life is felt on both sides of the arbitrary division, and the scope for living is limited within, as well as between, the several segments.[1]

Under present conditions the individuals found to suffer most consistently in school are children of minority status. If club membership is determined by academic achievement or if pupils are classified according to verbal tests, more boys and girls from some minority backgrounds than from majority backgrounds tend to be found among the excluded or retarded ones. This conspicuousness as a group usually results in lowered prestige for each member of the minority in question, in his own eyes as well as in those of everybody else. Then fear and a sense of futility may easily become

[1] That the problem of sectioning and separation is receiving wide discussion is evidenced by an article which appeared in the *New York Times* concerning the report sponsored by the Rockefeller Brothers Fund on United States educational needs:

". . . it [the report] repeatedly stressed that the individual's talents must be developed 'in a context of concern for all.'

"The report eschewed the philosophy behind Rear Admiral Hyman G. Rickover's suggested elite academies for the intellectually gifted. It opposed the idea of separating students by ability. In a democracy, the panel said, there is much to be gained by mixing bright and slow and in-between in the same classes. Let good teachers challenge each according to his abilities.

"Likewise, the European single-test system of selecting students was rejected. While repeated testings of the elementary grades were recommended, the report's words were strong to the effect that no tests yet devised could measure two of the three ingredients of superior performance: Motivation and character."

(From Loren B. Pope, reporting on *The Pursuit of Excellence: Education and the Future of America,* prepared by Panel V of the Special Studies Project of the Rockefeller Brothers Fund, in *New York Times,* June 23, 1958, p. 16.)

chronic states of mind for such students and may undercut their hopes and self-confidence from the beginning. The consequences may be just as unfortunate for the girls and boys from the cultural majority. It is in this sort of social context that ideas are generated about the superiority of certain races and the inadequacy or undesirability of others.

Until recently schools have not had reliable means for studying the social interaction of children and have thus hardly been in a position to use fully the laboratory at their disposal for educational ends. But as soon as social relations can be studied, they can also be guided and enriched. With the help of relatively simple instruments, it is now possible to develop such group life in school as will engage the interests of the participants in one another, widen mutual appreciation and psychological exchange, provide maximum opportunity for the satisfaction of varying individual capacities, and promote the stimulus and satisfactions possible through joint action.

The object of this report is to describe a method of studying the interaction of children so that teachers may not only become more fully aware of existence of interaction, but also may build on it for educational purposes. In the next chapter the sociometric method, as it is called, is presented in considerable detail to cover some of the instruments and methods of interpreting and applying the results obtained.

II. THE SOCIOMETRIC TEST

SOCIOMETRY IS THE STUDY OF THE PATTERNS OF INTERRELATIONS between people and the process of their measurement. It is not concerned with official relationships but with the psychological components of interactive relationships. The main instrument, the sociometric test, discloses the feelings which individuals have regarding one another *in respect to* membership in the group in which they are at a given moment—ideally, all groups in which they are members. (It is often erroneously described as a test of friendship constellations.)[1]

Sociometric technique is the use of appropriate sociometric tests to reveal group structure and to identify subdivisions of the group and various types of group positions, for example, leaders, isolates, rival factions, and so on.[2] A sociogram is a graph used for presenting simply the structure of the relations at a given time among members of a given group. The major lines of communication, or the pattern of attraction and rejection in its broad scope, are made readily comprehensible at a glance.

In school the information for making up the sociogram is obtained by asking the children to choose from among themselves preferred companions for some in-school situation that is real to them. The results are the data for the sociogram.

It is next necessary to use interviews and other methods in order to gain understanding of the motives and values underlying the choices and rejections. Each sociogram is thus only a starting point for further investigation but it does indicate in what directions investigation is most needed. A series of sociograms at stated intervals, with follow-up studies as indicated, is needed before a

[1] H. H. Jennings, "Sociometry," in Philip Lawrence Harriman (ed.), *Encyclopedia of Psychology* (New York: Philosophical Library, 1946), p. 874.
[2] Carter V. Good (ed.), *Dictionary of Education* (New York: McGraw-Hill Book Co., 1945), p. 379.

particular classroom "society" may be properly understood.[3] As a starting point, however, the chief significance of a sociogram lies in its comprehensive revelation of the group structure at one time in its development.[4]

THE DISTINCTIVENESS OF SOCIOGRAMS

Many ways of studying interaction among pupils have been tried, and many teachers are familiar with most of them. For instance, much can be learned from direct observation: who usually plays with whom, who whispers to whom, who walk home together, or who accompany whom at school events. Similar information often comes from hearsay and from the reports of other people. Whether deliberately asked for or not, teachers regularly get valuable leads about their pupils from remarks children make about each other, from what other teachers say, or from comments of their parents, their club leaders, or other members of the community. Sometimes much can be learned from the girls and boys themselves. Still another index of social relations is furnished by the list of formal associations: who belongs to what club, who is elected to what office, who is always in everything, and who never seems to take part.

All these sources can provide some degree of insight. But the information gained from observation, hearsay, and student records is at best only partial. Frequently it is highly selective and, consequently, distorted. For this reason it can be of more help after, rather than before, a sociometric analysis has been made. The above sources of data cannot show, for instance, how each individual child would like to associate or how his wishes compare with

[3] Hilda Taba and Deborah Elkins, *With Focus on Human Relations: A Story of an Eighth Grade* (Washington: American Council on Education, 1950). This publication illustrates the group life understandings and insights into individuals which systematic use of sociometric procedures in conjunction with curriculum and other follow-up procedures can achieve and, specifically, the kinds of growth promoted.

[4] Hilda Taba, *With Perspective on Human Relations* (Washington: American Council on Education, 1955). This publication, which has the subtitle *A Study of Peer Group Dynamics in an Eighth Grade* is based upon further extensive analysis of data from the study by Taba and Elkins cited above. The two books are complementary, covering different aspects of the research. Also, both are so concrete in explanation and description that any teacher may use them as guides to doing similar work in her own class.

the feelings of others toward him. They do not map the cross-currents and over-all interlocking of relations. Even though teachers do locate certain affinities and dislikes accurately without the help of sociometry, they still have no way of knowing who may have wanted to join a group and who was left out, or did not know how to go about it, or was afraid of being rebuffed. Moreover, unsystematic observation is usually accurate only at the extremes—it spots some of the highly chosen children and some who are left out. It tends to be most inaccurate in the middle range of children who are not conspicuously chosen or left out.

The distinctive characteristic of sociometric methods, accordingly, is their capacity to describe a complete picture of spontaneous interaction in the whole range of its manifestation in relation to important criteria of group life. Sociometric methods focus attention on the dynamic aspects of interaction rather than on individual children in isolation from one another.

ADMINISTERING THE SOCIOMETRIC TEST

The spontaneous choice of associates is the index used in the sociometric test, by which it describes social relations. To protect this spontaneity, it is important to keep all steps in administering the test informal and to make them real to the boys and girls. In other words, students must fully understand that the question is asked in order to be useful to them and that their personal reaction is important because they are to benefit from the consequences. Accordingly, rapport with children is a prerequisite for using sociometric procedures. Conditions likely to elicit genuine response must be maintained in the selection of the test situation and in the method of administering it.

Selecting the test situation

The test situation must offer children opportunities for choice that are meaningful as well as natural to them. The first criterion, then, is to choose situations which can be acted upon and the consequences of which matter to the children. Such situations as choosing companions for sitting together in homerooms or class, for working together on committees, or for carrying out projects together in small groups have been found useful for this purpose.

Furthermore, it is well to take advantage of whatever is familiar or customary in a particular classroom. If the girls and boys are used to breaking up into small committees, then it is easy to ask them with whom each would prefer to work. In almost all rooms the question of seating arrangements is important. Or, some teachers may prefer to build on the enthusiasm developed by some new experience, such as a class trip or planning a party, and ask for associates for this purpose. In all cases, the context must be such that the test results have immediate practical significance for the children. It must be possible to carry out the original agreement with them on the basis of which they made their choices.

Opportunities for choice should also be selected according to their relative freedom from inhibiting factors. The girls and boys should be in a position, as much as possible, to follow their full inclinations without regard to any other factors. For example, suppose an auditorium has to be used as a study hall and it has been the practice to ask boys and girls to work in different parts of it, then it would be inadvisable to use the question of seating arrangements in this context for sociometric purposes because the choices across sex lines might be inhibited. The established pattern will inevitably be reflected: girls will ask to sit next to girls, and boys will choose boys, much more frequently than if they had not been used to separated arrangement. The experience of the project shows that whatever restrictions exist in the surroundings will influence the children's choices. If the object is to get at real inclinations in order to have the basis for diagnosing human relations, then care must be exercised to free the situation of inhibiting factors.

Occasionally one may wish to use the sociogram in order to diagnose the effect of changing rules and arrangements, such as would be the case when a school, after seating boys and girls apart in auditorium and lunchroom, has undertaken to mix them. Under these conditions the situations in which change is taking place can be used for sociometric purposes, provided a little time is allowed to elapse so that the children learn to give free rein to their feelings. A series of sociograms then, at suitable intervals every few months or so, will show a gradual relaxation of the former pattern as the boys and girls become used to the idea that it is "all right" for them to choose across sex lines or the barriers of ethnic or cultural background.

Wording the sociometric question

After selecting the test situation, it is important to get the children to express themselves as spontaneously as possible in their choices of associates. The teacher should make it quite clear that the class is actually to be reseated, or the committees set up, or the proposed plans carried out, and also for how long the new arrangement is to last. It should likewise be explained that nobody except the teacher will see or use the results, that it will not necessarily be possible to give everybody his first choice of associate when there are thirty or forty pupils to satisfy, but that every effort will be made to see that each pupil will be with one classmate of his choice and more than one whenever possible. However, the teacher should be very careful not to say or hint anything about how to choose; the object is to get genuine reaction. It is best not to use the term "sociometric test," even with high school students, since it sounds formidable and the word "test" is associated with right and wrong answers of some sort.

To administer the test question, the teacher should pass out blank slips of paper or 3- x 5-inch cards, on which the children are asked to write their own names in the upper left corner and the names of their choices one by one below. The wording of the question determines in very large measure the usefulness of the results. It is, therefore, highly desirable to follow some well-tried procedure, such as the following statement used by a high school teacher of social studies:

We are going to need committees to work on — and — problems. Each of you knows with whom you enjoy working most. These may be the same people with whom you work in other classes, or they may be different, so remember that we are talking about social studies. Put your name at the top of the page and numbers 1, 2, and 3 on lines below. Opposite "1" put the name of a boy or girl with whom you would most like to work, after "2" your second choice, and after "3" your third. I will keep all of the choices in mind and arrange the committees so that everyone will be with one or more of the three people named. Remember, you may choose a boy or girl who is absent today if you want to. Write down the last names as well as the first names so that I'll be sure to know whom you mean. As usual, we shall probably be working in these committees for about eight weeks, or until the Christmas holidays.

Remember I said your committees will be so arranged that you will be with one or more of the boys or girls you choose. So it's best you keep your choices confidential. Since it's impossible to place every person so that he has all his choices, you will be with some who have chosen you and whom you may not have chosen. You wouldn't want such people to think you hadn't considered them when perhaps you would have chosen them for your committee if you'd had more than three choices.

If the class has not been accustomed to working in small groups, the teacher might begin differently: "Each of you has a pretty good idea of whom you would like to work with most. Let's try a new way to set up groups of people who want to work together, by forming committees." And so forth, according to the specific situation in the classroom and the nature of the choice offered.

The immediate possibilities for sociometric grouping will vary in different settings. Thus, in homerooms one arrangement may be for seating, another arrangement for committees, although the same children are involved.

An example of one kind of question which some schools use at change of semesters to compose their homerooms on the basis of pupil's choices follows:

What other boys or girls do you want to be in the *same* homeroom with you next semester? You may give three choices, naming the boy or girl you *most* want to be grouped with you as your first choice, then the one you want as second choice, and as third choice. It's hard to arrange enrollment for all choices by each person, but everyone will have at least one of his choices. We should keep our choices confidential because some people will be choosing you whom you may not have chosen since you had only three choices.

Classroom seating is always important.[5] For the purpose of seating students according to their choices, they can be addressed in the following fashion:

You are seated now as you happened to get seated in our homeroom [state whatever the classroom is], but now that we all know one another, every pupil should have the opportunity to sit near other pupils he most wants to sit beside. Then the classroom can be arranged to

[5] See pp. 14, 33, 44, 48, 51, 56, 85–86, 91–93.

suit everyone. Write your own name and under it three choices of pupils you would like to sit near in this room. Put a "1" next to your first choice, a "2" for your second, and a "3" for your third choice. I will try to fit in as many of everyone's choices as possible. But since there are many pupils and each of you may be choosing in many different ways, you can see that I can only do my best to arrange the seats so that everyone gets at least one choice, and more choices only if I can figure the seats out that way.

Choices can be appropriately used for arrangement or rearrangement of the life situation of individuals only when they are expressed in relation to a specific situation. The emphasis is on *the activity* or *situation* and on which persons the individual would *most enjoy* or *want* to be with. The choice of persons and situation are linked *in one statement*. The specific situation or activity is the criterion: it is what makes the choosing question socio*metric,* measuring as it does the structure of relationships for the specific setting. The word "friend" or similar expression (as, "like best") is to be avoided; it provides no criterion and is unsuitable further because it may be inhibiting and confusing to the chooser as well as inexact for sociometric purposes.

If the children are too young to write for themselves, as in the primary grades, they may be asked to give their choices orally. Care must be taken that each child has the opportunity to tell the teacher of his or her choices well out of hearing of the other children. Plenty of time must be allowed, depending on how quickly the particular children respond. Usually some five minutes or less will be found sufficient.

Frequently it is appropriate and desirable, on the same occasion, to ask for the names of any classmates with whom a child may prefer not to work or sit near, or whatever the situation is. This is particularly important when tensions are known to exist, and there is unusual need for complete diagnosis. Many of the otherwise unaccountable failures of group work become clear and understandable once the full picture of interpersonal relations is established. In this connection, no implication should be allowed to creep in that one person is asked to judge another; the emphasis belongs on the two-way nature of whatever negative feelings are to be expressed. The teacher's manner should be matter of fact, direct, and natural—not indirect, vague, or apologetic. Some such statement as the following, to be given after the choices are made, is appropriate:

Each of you also knows if there are any people with whom you would feel particularly uncomfortable on this committee for [use the situation of the sociometric test], or who may feel that way about you. I can arrange your work to avoid this. If there are any with whom you would rather not be, or who you think feel the same way about you, put their names at the bottom of the paper. If there aren't, leave it blank.

The teacher should be sure that everyone has given three choices, but no specific number of rejections should be asked for or even implied. Sometimes a child chooses the teacher or says "anyone will do." It is desirable to try to get such children to make another statement. If the child still demurs, then there is no point in pressing further. Usually such students respond to a personal request, such as:

You may not be sure whom you want to work with most, but at least you can make a better guess than I. Won't you just do the best you can? Anyway, the choices are not forever—just for the next eight weeks [state agreed period]; then you'll have a chance to choose again. By choosing now and being with some of those you choose, you'll discover whether you really do enjoy these particular people. In case you find they aren't quite the ones for you, you may make different choices next time. In our arrangement you learn about yourself, then, as well as about other people.

Teachers should always feel free to answer any questions that may occur to the group, both before and during the writing. The most important things to remember about administering the test are: (1) to include the motivating elements in the introductory remarks, (2) to word the question so that children understand how the results are to be used, (3) to allow enough time, (4) to emphasize *any* boy or girl so as to approve in advance any direction the choice may take, (5) to present the test situation with interest and some enthusiasm, (6) to say how soon the arrangements based on the test can be made, and (7) to keep the whole procedure as casual as possible.

Whatever the particulars of the specific sociometric test, it must live up to the following criteria if it is to fulfill its function: The basis of the choice must be real and not hypothetical. The test itself must be a means for some actual purpose, never an end in itself. The results are to be carried out in arrangements for living as wanted by all the members. The application is immediate; the action is taken to be effective at once—tomorrow or next week, but not at some vague time in the future.

Although it seldom happens that children tell one another whom they have chosen, having been told it is inadvisable to do so, there may occasionally occur instances involving a few children who are so excitable or anxious to communicate the information that they do tell others whom they have chosen. Under these circumstances the teacher, upon hearing of it, should repeat to the class the obligation of privacy among themselves, but should not focus attention upon the violators or speak especially to them; should they approach her, she should state her trust that they will remember next time and acknowledge that it is easy to forget the first time. She should, in speaking to the class as a whole, remind the pupils that she has the same obligation not to tell a parent or any pupil who might ask.

The total results of the sociometric testing are held, of course, totally confidential; neither children nor parents are given any specific information or permitted to see the sociogram.

The degree of intimacy that exists between the pupils and teacher and between parents and teacher will determine how the teacher answers inquiries. She can explain to all that it is important that each of us grow in his use of choice, discover what people he enjoys, and learn to take social initiative; that, in order to gain practice in such matters, one must feel free to be sincere; and that if one has to account to anyone, this feeling of freedom may be reduced, Further, it may be explained that the very nature of the grouping requires that the choices be kept confidential; for, in order to carry out the agreement that everyone will receive at least one of his choices, it will seldom be possible to give even one person all three of his choices. Since this means that each student will probably be grouped with some persons who have chosen him but whom he has not chosen, choices must be kept confidential so that no one will be put in doubt about being wanted in his group.

MAKING THE SOCIOGRAM

As already noted, the children's responses may be written either on slips of paper or on 3- x 5-inch cards. Some teachers find cards easier to handle since they provide a uniform set of materials with which to work. However, no matter what method is used, great care must be taken to see that the children do not come across any of the material later. For this reason it may be safer to enter all information on a tabulation form, such as the sample illustrated in Figure 1 (page 21), and then destroy the original slips.

If the teacher prefers to work directly on the cards, he can enter the choices each child receives to the right, indicating by a number after the chooser's name the order of the choice. Rejections may be entered in the same way, separated from the choices by a line. Thus, those on the left would be read as the child's own choices and rejections, and those on the right as the choices and rejections he may have received from other children. When all responses have been entered on the cards, the sociogram may be put together directly from the data. Some teachers, when they wish to make up committee groups or devise combinations of children to work or play together, select the cards for each child involved, clip the several cards together, and thus have for ready reference a record of the arrangement they wish to foster when a particular situation arises.

On the other hand, some teachers find it more advantageous to use a form such as that illustrated in Figure 1. The spaces across the top are to be used to indicate the names of the pupils chosen, and those along the left side are for entering the names of the children making the choices; the names of all in the group should accordingly appear in both places. If Joseph Gold has chosen John Smith, Ruth Allis, and Irene Brown, in that order (to use the example on the form), the first thing to do is to find Joseph Gold to the left and then, staying on his row, to insert a number "1" below the name of John Smith, a "2" below that of Ruth Allis, and a "3" below Irene Brown. The square under each pupil's own name across the top and on his own row from the left can be blocked out straight down the page, since the child will not choose himself. The sum of the choices received in each category (first, second, third) may then be recorded for each person at the bottom of the form in the spaces provided.

SOCIOMETRIC TABULATION FORM

Chosen → / Chooser ↓	Ruth Allis	Irene Brown						Jos. Gold										John Smith		
Ruth Allis	·																			
Irene Brown		·																		
			·																	
				·																
					·															
						·														
							·													
Jos. Gold	2	3						·										1		
									·											
										·										
											·									
												·								
													·							
														·						
															·					
																·				
																	·			
John Smith																		·		
																			·	
																				·
Chosen as:																				
1st choice																		1		
2nd choice	1																			
3rd choice		1																		
TOTAL																				

FIG. 1.—Sociometric Tabulation Form. List names in the same order vertically and horizontally. Insert a "1," "2," "3" in the proper squares to indicate the order of choices. Note example in the form: Joseph Gold chooses John Smith first, Ruth Allis second, and Irene Brown third.

The tabulation form is mainly useful in giving a total picture of all children's responses and all positions in the group. Furthermore, it is easy to lift from it the information needed when filling in the tally of sociometric positions for further analysis.

As teachers fill in the information either on the cards or a tabulation form, many questions will occur to them. How many mutual or reciprocated choices are there? Which individuals and what proportion of the class are very much in demand? What proportion is ignored? Do girls and boys choose each other? Are there any reciprocated choices across sex lines? And many more. The form illustrated in Figure 2 is designed to help answer such questions and suggest others that the teacher may not have thought of. It will be seen that spaces are provided for tabulating the number of choices each child may have received according to such significant group factors as sex, race, or place of residence. The relative demand for each individual, the number of mutual choices, and any unusual patterns of association will also be indicated. When space is needed for choices going outside the group, an additional column can be made to the right on the form.

If groups are compared with each other, some common measure such as a percentage is needed. While there are as yet no established norms with which to compare a group of a given age level and sex composition, there are certain frequencies of choice distribution, based on results of tests of large populations in kindergarten through the eighth grade, which may be useful in gaining perspective on the developmental trends of children, shown in the tabulation below.

But important and interesting though it is to find out the sociometric position of each individual child, it is perhaps even more

ANALYSIS OF SOCIOMETRIC CHOICES BY GRADES*

(Averaged from Two Tests Given 22 Months Apart on a Population of About 2,000, Public School 181, Brooklyn, N.Y.)

Grade Level	Percent of Choices between Boys and Girls	Percent of Unchosen Children	Percent of Mutual Choice Pairs
Kindergarten	26.0	31.0	6.5
1st grade	24.3	28.0	7.0
2nd grade	21.1	28.5	12.5
3rd grade	14.1	27.5	14.0
4th grade	5.7	21.5	18.0
5th grade	4.7	18.0	19.0
6th grade	2.6	17.5	19.0
7th grade	3.2	20.5	21.0
8th grade	4.8	19.0	16.5

* J. L. Moreno, *Who Shall Survive?* (New York: Beacon House, 1934), pp. 26-27. The data given in this table show magnitudes similar to those obtained by J. Criswell in a later study, "Sociometric Analysis of Negro-White Groups," *Sociometric Review*, 1936, pp. 50-53. Both pieces of research are based on two-choice allowance.

TALLY OF SOCIOMETRIC POSITIONS

No. of Boys_____ ; No. of Girls_____

Class/Grade_____
School_____
City_____
Date Given_____

Test Question:_____
How many choices were asked for?____ . Total number of choices made by all students?____
Maximum number of choices posible (multiply size of group by number of choices allowed)____

Enter in the spaces below the number of pupils holding each position listed.

Frequency of Choice	NUMBER OF PUPILS			
	Chosen	Chosen Mutually	Rejected*	Rejected Mutually*
Not at all	____	____	____	____
Once	____	____	____	____
Twice	____	____	____	____
Three times	____	____	____	____
Four times	____	____	____	____
Five times	____	____	____	____
More than 5 times . .	____	____	____	____
TOTAL NO. OF PUPILS† .	____	____	____	____

SAMPLE BREAKDOWNS OF TALLY OF POSITIONS ALONG GROUP FACTOR LINES‡

Frequency of Choice	No. of Choices Received		No. of Choices Received		No. of Choices Received	
	Boys	Girls	Negro	White	Live in Housing Project	Do Not Live in Housing Project
None	____	____	____	____	____	____
One	____	____	____	____	____	____
Two	____	____	____	____	____	____
Three	____	____	____	____	____	____
Four	____	____	____	____	____	____
Five	____	____	____	____	____	____
Total by category . .	____	____	____	____	____	____
TOTAL NO. OF PUPILS	____	____	____	____	____	____

FURTHER QUESTIONS

How many boys chose girls and were not reciprocated?_____
[Or, e.g., how many white children chose Negro children and were not reciprocated?]
How many girls chose boys and were not reciprocated?_____
Number of mutual choices between boys and girls._____

SPECIAL FEATURES

Note here any pattern which is of especial interest to you, e. g., "Three of the unchosen pupils chose the same much-chosen pupil."_____

*Enter only if a rejection question was used.
†Totals of each column should equal the number of children in the group.
‡Positions may be broken down into whatever categories for analysis will disclose whether particular group factors are operating to affect its structures.

FIG. 2.—Tally of Sociometric Positions. In preparing his own forms, the teacher may substitute whatever categories are appropriate for breaking down the tally of positions and whatever further questions he may be particularly interested in.

significant from the standpoint of educational implications to study the social structure of the class as a whole. The results of the test are thus given graphic presentation. Figure 3 displays a sample sociogram form on which choices have been entered. The circles symbolize girls, and the triangles, boys.

Beginning with the girls' half of the form, the circles nearest the center should be used for frequently chosen children; the circles nearest them should be assigned to mutual-choice girls—that is, who have chosen each other. The more distant circles may be used as needed for girls who have been given a few or no choices. The name of each pupil should be printed in full inside the appropriate symbol. The boys' half of the sociogram is then filled out in the same manner.

On forms to be used in the primary grades, the circles and triangles may be mixed together, for young children make their choices without much reference to sex. If the object is to study .developmental patterns all through the grades, it is easier to watch the gradual drawing-away and the later coming-together again between girls and boys when the same sociogram form is used throughout.

The sample sociogram (Figure 3) shows how these various items are entered. Choices between children are indicated by lines drawn in the following manner: An unreciprocated, or one-way, choice is shown by an arrow from the chooser pointing to the chosen person. The degree of this choice is indicated by placing the appropriate number at the base of the line from the symbol for the chooser. A one-way choice is illustrated by Paula King's choice of Saul Tonik. A mutual choice is shown by a line *touching* the symbols for both choosers with a small vertical bar at the center of the connecting line and the appropriate choice number placed at the base of the line of the chooser; arrows are not needed in this case. This is illustrated by Gale Keyne and Janet Toll. A dotted symbol should be used for any absent person. This situation is illustrated by Joe Brown. If rejections are obtained, they may be indicated in the same way except that the lines are made in short dashes or in a different color.

The speediest method for making the sociogram, however, and one which is equally satisfactory (and, hence, preferred by the

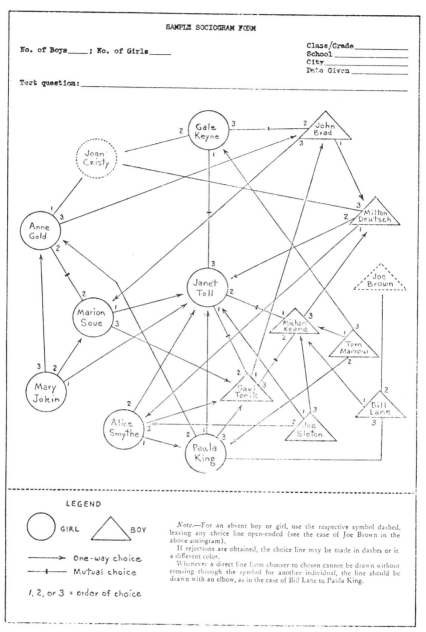

FIG. 3.—A filled-in sociogram form, presenting graphically the choice patterns. Blank forms, with empty circles and triangles, may be mimeographed so that the teacher may fill in the names and draw in the choice lines after the test has been given.

writer) is to construct it directly from the choice slips. By flipping rapidly through the slips, one can note which boys and girls are very frequently chosen; since many lines of choice will be coming to them, their names can be placed in the central area of the sociogram. One by one, the information on each choice slip can be fully entered by placing in convenient spots the names mentioned and leaving unfinished the return response until the choice slip of that individual is reached. Since the most-chosen persons have already been located in the central area, care need be taken only in locating other individuals in such manner as to keep the sociogram readily readable. For examples of good technique in this respect, see Figures 5–11, which also show that girls are placed to the left and boys to the right to aid the reading of volume of intersex choices.

FOLLOWING UP THE CLUES

To a person looking at a sociogram for the first time, the whole thing may seem to be a meaningless jumble of circles, lines, and triangles. The first problem, then, is to find the pattern and gradually see its significance. After a little practice, sociograms can be read for major outlines or characteristic shape at a glance, and study is called for only in connection with details or the interaction of individual children. Once the picture is firmly in mind, or, indeed, while it is actually taking shape, all sorts of questions will suggest themselves for further study.

Reading the sociogram

A good way to begin reading a sociogram is to concentrate on one person and follow all lines that lead from and to him. In the sample shown in Figure 3, the circle marked "Mary Jokin" in the lower left corner has three arrows (unreciprocated choices) running from it to Janet Toll (first), Marion Soue (second), and Anne Gold (third). There are no arrows pointing at Mary; she has not received a single choice. Looking at Janet, we find that her first choice is a boy, Saul Tonik, and it is reciprocated as Saul's second possibility; her second choice is another boy, Michael Keane, and is also reciprocated—she is first on Michael's list; her third choice is again reciprocated, by a girl this time, Gale Keyne, and represents another first choice. In addition, there are six arrows pointing at Janet, coming from two boys and four girls; moreover, four of these are first choices and the others second choices. Everyday life in the classroom must obviously be very different for Janet and Mary!

On looking further at the sociogram for any other patterns, a mutual choice will be discovered between Saul and Michael—the two boys who chose Janet. Here is a triangle established on the basis of mutual choices on all three sides. Another pair relation exists between Janet's choice, Gale, and John Brad, and still another between Anne and Marion, both of whom had been vainly chosen by Mary. Other sociograms might show additional triangles or squares or pentagons of mutual choices, dividing the class into two or more clearly defined groups. If these patterns of relation are completely self-contained with no arrows or lines running between them, it means that friendship goes by cliques. But that would be an extreme situation. The most frequently encountered pattern within the over-all network is a sort of string or chain of one-way choices; there is a twisting line on the sample sociogram running from Mary to Anne to John to Milton to Alice to Janet. Even in the primary grades such chains occur relatively often and are sometimes very long.

Once the lines have begun to fall into shape, many surprises are likely to emerge. Certain pupils turn out to have been chosen, or overlooked, or rejected in a way that few adults would have predicted. A common surprise of this sort is the unexpected degree to which some gentle, quiet child who is "not doing very well in class" is chosen. What do his classmates see in him? And why do they select him to work with on a project? Some choices, on the other hand, are perfectly understandable at first glance. That Saul, for instance, has a way with grown-ups and children alike; besides, he is unassuming and always cheerful and very helpful to everybody. On second thought, he is so very pleasant to have around that maybe he ought to have been chosen even more conspicuously than he actually was. Active, energetic students are sometimes wanted to an exceptional degree, and sometimes they are not.

Some children ask only for companions whose interests seem very different from their own or who are temperamentally very different and, one would have thought, not very sympathetic to them. "Ornery fellows" who ask to be with quiet children come to mind in this connection, as does the timid boy who wrote down as his first choice the "spoiled" son of well-to-do parents. But opposites do not invariably attract each other; sometimes it is definitely like to like. Some common factors will stand out also. For example, the fact that four children have made choices only among themselves may turn out to be related to the circumstance that they all come from a "tough" neighborhood and have felt obliged to band together in self-defense; or perhaps their mothers have been lifelong friends and the children accept the expectation that they too should be friends. There may, of course, be other reasons—especially if the closed group represents one ethnic group or socio-economic level of the population and differs in this respect from the rest of the class. Somebody may have been left unchosen because he was quite unknown as an individual in the school or because his background was strange and his personality misunderstood. Sometimes choices have been governed by the value put on certain skills—in athletic or even academic achievement—and the school records will confirm the children's assessment. But again, children's choices may have been controlled by some standard of their own, the influence of which may have been sensed in interviews but which must be studied in more situations before it is understood.

The configuration made by a sociogram as a whole should be noted for the comprehensive information it gives about the patterns of interaction. One of these is the chain already described. Chains appear in sociograms for all grades, but they differ considerably from one level to another, in length and in the number of mutual choices in the links. The longer the chain, the longer, also, the line of communication. If, however, hardly any chain extends beyond three or four children, it means that little opportunity is available for ventilation either of ideas or influences. The teacher may want to look for occasions to establish contacts between the separate networks. Once it is clear where these are needed, much effort which otherwise would be aimed vaguely at developing group spirit can be precisely focused on aiding different sets of children to know one another. Obviously, the more links that are fostered among pupils, the more opportunities the teacher will have for grouping them congenially.

If chains are long, connecting perhaps most of the pupils, it will be clear why the class acts as if in one accord when one member seems to be in difficulty or some idea gets started. Such a broad network will be helpful when group consideration is needed. There is also likely to be a spread of leadership. Hence, it can be expected that the group as a whole will show signs of caring about what happens to any member. The teacher can count on getting cooperation from various pupils. An instance of this happening in such a classroom may be cited here. A certain pupil had been doing very little work and not taking seriously his teacher's warning about possible failure. In order to impress upon him what it would be like not to be with his own class, she asked him to spend a few days in the grade below his. This happened just before noon dismissal. Upon returning to class that afternoon the teacher received a petition signed by every child except the culprit. It read: "Joseph is our class member. It's our fault as much as his if he doesn't work. Please let him stay with us. We will see that he does." In the light of the interrelations indicated by the pupils' choices, the teacher was confident that the class as a group could give such aid. Group effort induced change in this student's behavior.

When the social structure appears to be integrated around a few children, with very little overlap among the pupils choosing each of them, it will be clear why the teacher will have sensed different sections of the class trying to block the interests of the others. In such cases, action may be taken to spread the network throughout the whole group. A good way to start is to set up an activity for which the child leaders will need assistance from one another. In so doing, the following of each youngster can be led to break down whatever code may have been built up about what other members can do.

When the sociogram simply looks shaggy, with hardly any focus at all, there is likely to be similar looseness and lack of direction in class activity. The teacher will have difficulty in organizing a group for joint effort unless opportunities are first provided for students to know each other and to use each other's talents. In other words, projects must be introduced that require looking at things together, necessitating a commonality of approach.

When the pattern shows sharp divisions of children who choose only their own set and neither give nor receive choices from outside, the clique pattern is indicated. There are likely to be antagonisms and disagreements among the pupils, and, consequently, lack of cooperation among different groups. The teacher may be faced with the problem not only of extending networks between the sets, but also of looking into what has caused the separations and what curriculum content will aid in counteracting such values as may have induced the separation.

In order to interpret fully what a sociogram means, it will be necessary to know many things about the children. The same line of study will not be called for in each case, but the following categories of information are generally found helpful. First, teachers need to know where their students live and something of their home background: Are there marked differences among them in socioeconomic circumstances? Are any groups set off from one another in family tradition, language, religion, or the like? Are certain cultural groups notably at a disadvantage numerically or in any other way? If there have been any recent newcomers, how do they compare with the others in these respects? Do any of the girls and boys experience any particular strains or unusual satisfactions out of school? Are any of them handicapped at all—physically, mentally, temperamentally, economically? Do any live in institutions or away from home for any reason?

Another important category of information has to do with local customs and traditions, both in school and in the community: Does the curriculum operate to keep certain groups apart—boys and girls, children of different racial backgrounds, residents of different neighborhoods? Are there any regulations or routine procedures that either block or direct association? Do these reflect community expectation? What about parental standards and prohibitions? And the like. Any or all of the factors suggested might significantly influence the pattern of the sociogram. Possibly some evidence will be disclosed of more or less conscious conflict between child values and the regulations or standards of adults.

And no matter how much information is collected, there will always be some questions that remain unanswered after all the above considerations have been weighed and checked.

In order to systematize this first reading of a sociogram and to make sure that relevant areas are identified for further investigation, the sociometric analysis schedule (below) may be useful. Some questions on this schedule call for the analysis of individuals, others are designed to reveal group factors. While certain questions cannot be answered without further study, others may be answered at once from such readily available information as health records, the results of intelligence and aptitude tests, academic records, club membership, cumulative files and anecdotal records, or notes on visits to homes and talks with parents, or from just what teachers happen to know about individuals. This pooling of explanations by a faculty group will bring more relevant considerations into play than if each teacher attempts to analyze her sociograms alone.

SOCIOMETRIC ANALYSIS SCHEDULE

1. What appears that you had expected would appear?
2. What appears that you had not expected to appear?
3. What seems to account for certain pupils being the most chosen and receiving few, if any, rejections?
4. What seems to account for certain pupils being unchosen or receiving many rejections?
5. What seems to account for the mutual choices?
6. What seems to account for the mutual rejections?
7. Can you think of any classroom arrangements which may account for the above choices or rejections?
8. As you read the structure as a whole, do you think of any arrangements such as classroom routines, lunchroom arrangements, play patterns, which might be a factor in the general patterning of the sociogram?
9. What cleavages, if any, appear in this sociogram? Cleavage is here defined as an absence of choices between individuals related to a "group factor." Examples: boy-girl, economic, nationality background, religious, academic ability, being employed after school, prestige of some special group, other group factors.
10. Can you see any spots in the structure of the group as a whole that need to be more closely related to the rest of the class group for better morale, such as a clique by itself, several mutually choosing children, other children trying to get in with no response?

11. In the light of your analysis of their interrelation structure, what understandings and skills do you estimate the pupils have already developed? Which do you estimate they need to develop further?
12. What do the majority of most-chosen children have in common? Examples: race; don't work after school; socioeconomic level, fairly well off; live in open community and not the housing project; most are Protestants; most have lived in this community all their lives; most take part in after-school and in-school activities.
13. What do the unchosen and rejected children have in common? Examples: different nationality; much lower socioeconomic level than the others; most live in housing project; many of them work after school; many are new to community; don't participate in in-school and out-of-school activities; present many discipline problems.
14. Are there visible signs of segmentalization in your community—association patterns which divide according to race, religion, residence location, or any other factor?

Even a cursory consideration of these questions reveals many interesting things. Usually, for example, teachers have found many surprises in the revealed pattern of choices. These differences between expectation and actual fact often reflect a difference in what the teacher and the children think important. For example, teachers tend to stress such attributes as academic achievement, cleanliness, neatness, or being well dressed, but there is seldom any correlation to be found between such factors and the degree to which any child is chosen. There are, of course, exceptions. For example, in a school where cliques were formed on the basis of socioeconomic status, dress was definitely an important consideration to the students. In contrast, in another school students had rebelled against pressure to make high marks, and a code of not accepting anyone with a high academic rating came into existence. A person singled out by the teacher as a bad example may become an object of rejection, or the reverse, depending on how the class feels about the teacher. In some classrooms, those used as good examples were unchosen. Sometimes mutual rejections have occurred between children with similar gifts, one of whom has had many chances to show his capacities while the other has not.

School arrangements often affect choice patterns. When some of the students are given authority over others in a manner considered unfair by the latter, cleavages are apt to develop between the group in authority and the other students. Separation in seating, such as placing the best students near the teacher or segregating bad students, sets up choice patterns in which both the good and the bad students tend to reject those with whom they are grouped, even though for different reasons. A similar example may be cited from a comparison of three classrooms, of which two had a fairly broad pattern of interrelationships, but the third was exceptional in the extent of its divisions and rejections. The faculty recalled that all three sets of students had come at the same time, that fall, from the same school. In the former school they had comprised two classrooms. In arranging them in the new situation, the administration had split them into three groups and had segregated into one classroom all those pupils who had seemed to be problems. The resulting class was extremely disorganized, and it was difficult to improve morale without regrouping them.

Sometimes, again, a very refined classification according to academic achievement or scores in reading is made the basis of seating arrangements. In such settings, rejections often appear not only at the lower end of the scale, but also among members at the upper end who feel pressed to outdo their fellows if they are to retain their positions.

A cleavage frequently found, but fairly easy to overcome, is that between boys and girls where physical arrangements—such as separate lunchrooms, separate entrances, or separate elections —have kept them apart and induced competition rather than collaboration. Among primary children even separate playgrounds often have to be eliminated before closer relations can be cultivated between boys and girls.

Newcomers are another common source of cleavage. Sometimes this condition is traceable to the high prestige attached to being an old resident, and thus requires revision in curriculum content to effect change. In the main, simple arrangements whereby newcomers can make contacts will aid appreciably. When, however, newcomers have not only their newness to overcome as a social hurdle but, in addition, live in a new housing project or are physically set apart in some other way, the cleavage may have to be seen in relation to its fuller community aspects before it can be understood. This is, of course, true also of differences in racial, ethnic, religious, or home background which sometimes divide children within the same classroom. Precise knowledge of the roots of such cleavages helps a teacher to take appropriate steps, either in curriculum emphasis or in classroom practice.

Leads from interviews

The sociogram lays bare only the structure of interrelation, but not the reasons why this structure is what it is. The sociogram shows, for example, which children are isolated or unchosen, but it cannot reveal the reasons for the choices made. It presents an interesting picture of social structure that can, with information from further explorations, be used either for individual adjustment or for the re-education of the class. Inner motivations, which give the choices qualitative meaning, must be discovered by using additional methods. At the same time, it goes without saying, the teacher's entire professional training and experience in child study, observation, and interpretation will be important in how she uses any technique, including interviewing.[6]

The sociometric material will also serve to raise important questions as to why certain patterns of relation do not appear, such as why, perhaps, minority children do not choose one another or choose one another exclusively. Sometimes the children's background is immediately reflected in the results; sometimes valuable clues are given that must be followed up before this background can be understood. Thus, teachers may become aware of certain distortions in the children's thinking—possibly in part stemming from the meagerness of their experience outside the school or to the beginnings of prejudice derived from the adult world. The way this and similar situations will be met or ignored depends on the educational purpose which a particular faculty accepts for itself. The educative strategy employed should, of course, be carefully developed on the basis of additional information.

One follow-up is to interview children on how they came to choose as they did. Since it is important to get psychologically reliable information and since children no more than adults feel

[6] For Teacher's Home Interview Schedule, see pp. 41–43.

fully free to reveal themselves to their teachers, tact and rapport are needed in conducting these interviews.

Several considerations need to be kept in mind in drawing out children in these interviews. Since, in school, children are apt to have been asked many questions implying criticism or censure, it is necessary to avoid such implication even in the form of the question. Instead of asking directly, "Why did you choose Jane?" it is better to say, "How did you happen to choose Jane?" Second, talking with children about their choices and rejections should carry no suggestion that they have to justify themselves. Anything they say should be treated seriously and as entirely acceptable. When children appear not to know what to say in the interview, it is better not to press them directly, but to shift to some indirect procedure such as saying, "When did you start to feel as you do about —————?"

In view of the foregoing, it will be clear that teachers need to motivate even their most casual interviewing for their pupils, and often to proceed quite slowly. It has been found that children readily accept and understand any direct, simply truthful statement, such as the following:

We shall be living together in our classroom for the rest of the year, and I want to know each one of you as well and as quickly as I can. I want to keep on arranging our groups the way you each would like, and it would help me to do this if I understood how particular boys and girls are important to other boys and girls. As you know, we don't have much time between classes or lesson periods, but I should like to use what little time there is to get to know you better. So as we go along, I hope to talk to each of you in turn about your choices, how you feel about them, and whatever you care to say to help me understand your feelings.

Such informal or even casual interviewing has some advantages over a systematic schedule, since the teacher can often seize an opportunity when certain pupils are most in the mood to talk. Second, the spontaneity of the situation works in favor of frankness and freedom. However, since this takes time and those children who have not yet been contacted are apt to become impatient, it is desirable to proceed a little more formally as soon as it can be arranged. While the class as a whole is occupied at written or other work, for example, the teacher can speak with the pupils individually; three periods at most should be found sufficient to cover a total class.

Up to and including the third grade, the pupils will give the teacher their choices individually in interview. The simplest procedure here is to follow the child's naming of his choices by saying: "So that I may understand how you feel about each one, please tell me how you happened to choose [give the name of the first choice]." And so on.[7]

Naturally children's responses vary, depending on their maturity and degree of articulateness. Children in the primary grades usually say little that helps in understanding their choices. They sometimes answer, "Because she has long curls," or "He has nice brown eyes," or sometimes, "Because she lives near me," or "He plays with me." Older children can be much more explicit, as the following examples show:

He's my size [smallest in the class] and everything. He's a real nice kid and can talk about a lot of things. That's all we do when we have time. Anything like the hockey game, movies we liked. We walk part way home.

He gets around more. He seems to have a better life, not as many worries as I have; well I wasn't picked [at start] to be on patrol. I get into trouble. I get too angry and excited. Everyone tells me I have to go to the Hebrew School when I don't want to. Everything's going a little better now I'm on patrol.

I think he's a lot of fun; he has that Italian talk; I like to hear that; he puts it on because he knows it makes me laugh.

I like a lot of kids especially Robert and his brother; they don't go bullying the smaller kids. They're big but friendly.

Many children show surprising insight into their own needs. The very much rejected pupil who chooses to work with a respected class leader "because he believes in me" will be often encountered. High school students often speak very fully about what they do or do not enjoy about their classmates. Yet even

---

[7] For particularly astute considerations on sociometric testing and research interpretation at the early childhood level through sixth grade, see Mary L. Northway and Lindsay Weld, *Sociometric Testing: A Guide for Teachers* (Toronto: University of Toronto Press, 1957).

the most meager remarks can be meaningful if the teacher already knows a good deal about the child in question.

The answers are a valuable source of information for getting at the motives, values, and circumstances that determined the pattern of choices disclosed by the sociogram. However, some simple scheme for classifying the data will be needed in order to disclose what is relatively common and what is uniquely individual in the children's reasons for choice. Since what is likely to be emphasized by one group may not be at all important to another, it is often useful to begin by reading the material over quickly and noting the responses given most often. The major categories for classifying the material may thus be derived specifically for each set of papers. For example, children often provide clues to their personal codes in such statements as "He is too bossy," "Acts like a sissy, scared to fight," "She helps everyone," or "She won't give everyone a chance." Such statements clearly belong together under one heading. Again, children often emphasize things they do together: "Sells newspapers with me" or "We walk home together." Sometimes there are a number of special circumstances to be noted, such as, "Where I live is far away and he is willing to wait for me mornings." Or it may be important to note prejudgments accepted from parents, as in the following case: "My father says to stay away from Italians; Joseph I never spoke to but that's why I didn't choose him." By using whatever categories actually come out of the data for making the final check for relative emphasis or frequency, the teacher can get sharper insight into the children's common patterns of thought and feeling.

Once the more common patterns are ready for review, it is possible to note discrepancies that exist between what the school may be aiming at and the patterns within which the children operate. These discrepancies may lie in concepts or social skills as well as in attitudes or overt behavior. For example, in one school emphasizing good relations between boys and girls, girls were discovered to reject other girls "because they go with boys." Also, while teachers tried to create an open and growing group situation, students tended to value oldness of one close relationship even when both parties had outgrown the original mutuality of interest. They found many of their pupils insisting that, "Once you have been friends, you have to stay friends forever," and rejecting other youngsters who had branched out toward new contacts as ones "who don't stick with you." Individuals were often dropped because "parents do not approve." The same teacher found that some children used rigid moral judgments of "good" and "bad" regarding other people, while she was working toward functional assessment of people and their behavior. These judgments were based on an unverified reputation of "bad behavior" and the notion that pupils who behave differently from others are "peculiar."

Such clues gave this teacher an idea about what to do. For example, one of the notions prevailing among the children was that when people feel differently about the same thing, they should just keep away from each other. The concept toward which the teacher worked held that people only increase the misunderstanding between them if they refuse to exchange ideas. She wanted them to discuss their differences and try to find out how each came to feel as he did.[8]

It is not always convenient or possible for teachers to take the time to interview every pupil personally, especially on each occasion when they have made choices. In that event, children may be asked to write down their reasons and to explain how their chosen classmates are important to them. Directions for this method, described below, may be shortened or expanded according to a particular situation as long as there is no loss in motivation for the pupils.

Directions for the written interview can be somewhat as follows:

Last time I talked to you personally. We have done a lot of writing since then, and I have been pleased to see that you are able to put down how you feel about things. I wish this time you could tell me in writing how you happened to choose each one. When you use an adjective, like saying a person is "nice," please describe a situation in which you felt the person did or said something that you consider nice, so that I will know what each one of you means. If you say, "He's nice to be with," for instance, just add something to show what you mean by that. Write just as fully as you can whatever you want to say about the girls and boys you have chosen, as well as about anyone you don't

---

[8] For an action method of attitude change, see H. H. Jennings, "Sociodrama as Educative Process," in C. Tryon (ed.), *Fostering Mental Health in Our Schools* (Washington: Association for Supervision and Curriculum Development, National Education Association, 1950), p. 260-85.

get along with so well and how that happens. These papers will be confidential.

Open questions and themes

Interviews can get at students' general reactions, but other devices are necessary for securing more precise information. Several have been found useful. Written assignments on such topics as "Three Wishes," "If I Had One Hundred Dollars," or "The Person I Would Like to Be," usually yield some of the dominant values, such as wanting to possess things as against wanting something grand to happen to other people. Such questions as "What I'd Like to Change about My Home" can bring out indications of the emotional climate at home, the particular ways in which there is security, understanding, companionship, or anxiety, barrenness, and rejection.

A teacher may want to know even more about how the child feels about himself and others and how he thinks they feel about him. This type of information can be secured by having him write on such open themes as "What I Like about Myself," "What Others Like about Me or Say They Do," "How I Criticize Myself," "How Others Criticize Me." For example, in one school where this set of themes was used in the ninth grade, most of the ninth-graders assessed themselves and others almost exclusively in terms of physical appearance, posture, hairdress, and similar external factors. They criticized in themselves many unchangeable physical attributes such as being "too short," or having "an awful long neck." This revelation threw light on the methods the children used for gaining status and suggested ways in which either the school or the community center could enlarge the basis for gaining satisfactions.

In other groups such analyses indicated that the children were receiving adverse criticism in their homes, that they were often severely penalized for actions they did not themselves regard as wrong, that things were expected of them quite out of line with their capacities, and that they were being constantly dictated to and interfered with by family and neighbors alike. These findings made it clear why the pupils resented their teachers telling them ("dictating," in their estimation) what to do in the school setting, where they could hope for different treatment. It provided some insight, also, into why groups of children acted in concert as if to gain strength through numbers, both in gang life outside of school and in carry-over activities in school. The teachers began to analyze social situations, to diagnose their pupils' social skills, and to enrich the content and basis of personal relations for their boys and girls.

Diaries

Accounts of activities and experiences for a given day or two days or a week end, kept by all members of a classroom, can yield information on the patterns of human relations and their specific content—the regimen of family life, or the relation between the child's aspirations and the satisfactions actually open to him in his daily routine. For example, in some cases the child's out-of-school time was found to be almost wholly planned for him, and he had very few occasions for making decisions on his own. In others, children were generally left to their own devices, spent much time "loafing because I didn't have anything to do and no one came along," and decided pretty much everything without adult aid. In several instances diaries revealed that children's out-of-school activities with their age peers were for the most part confined to associating in small groups and randomly seeking diversion or doing the same activity over and over again. Rarely were out-of-school activities found to provide an occasion, either, for the children to engage in continuing activities of the sort requiring planning and skills for functioning in large groups.

The importance of data from themes, diaries, and other sources can be seen in the main only when each item is looked at in relation to the rest in order to build up the specific picture of the kinds of lives children lead.

Home interviews

Many of the factors that determine a child's place in the social structure of school life are rooted in the emotional and practical regimen of the family and in the quality of whatever family relations he enjoys or endures. Visits to homes can provide teachers with some idea of how a child's family setting may be aiding or blocking his happiness and growth.

For teachers who want to assess the environment in which the child lives, the Home Interview Schedule (below) will be useful. Each question has been set up to help get at the child's affectional status, the values his parents are inducing in him or expecting the school to encourage, and the parents' estimate of the child's reactions, all as a primary focus; the physical home setting and what physical necessities are at the child's disposal are considered from the standpoint of how the parent sees them. The form is aimed at avoiding the usual implications of teacher interviews that the school is prying into the child's private life in order to judge him.

TEACHER'S HOME INTERVIEW SCHEDULE[9]

INSTRUCTIONS

The interviewing schedule is for use in a personal interview with the child's parent (or parents) and to obtain a picture of the practical situation and *emotional* regime.

The schedule as a whole is constructed to aid the teacher to see what needs of the child are being met partially or fully in his home and so that the school can better plan for the child's development. It includes questions to disclose the parent's active efforts to build his values into the child's thinking and activities. It "leaves the door wide open" for the parent to offer help to the program of the school.

Information on physical home setting (number of rooms, etc.) and physical necessities (diet, clothing, water facilities) is mainly to be gathered incidentally from observation by the teacher while interviewing. Asking for such facts when these are not offered is not desirable. Question 8 is the only question directly bearing on the facilities of the home, and even here, unless the parent volunteers specific information, it is suggested that whatever kind of answer he gives is important if it shows how he feels about the level of standard of living he has at present.

In opening the interview the parent should be given the reasons why he is asked for an interview. For example: "Our school is conducting a study of its pupils so that the school may have more knowledge of what pupils need. We are asking you to give us about an hour. I have fourteen questions which will help us understand your viewpoints as a mother [father]. I am to take suggestions of different parents back to the school to help improve the program for your child and other children."

The teacher should have with her only the list of questions and a pad of paper. What the parent says should be recorded as nearly as possible in the parent's own words.

The nature of the questions assumes that the teacher will show an understanding, interested attitude and will listen carefully, never hurrying the parent. The questions invite the parent to reveal very intimate feelings and thoughts

---

[9] If for some reason little time is available and selection of questions is necessary, questions 1, 5, 7, 10, and 11 are suggested.

about his child, the school, the neighborhood, etc. Consequently, the teacher's important task is to establish such rapport that the parent will give information of value and also will afterwards be glad to cooperate with the school.

Throughout, the teacher should use his judgment about the order in which he gives the questions. Although the present order is usually found desirable, whenever it seems that the parent "isn't ready" for a given question, one which seems better at the time should be asked. In no case should the parent be pressed to answer.

In closing the interview the teacher should be certain the parent realizes his giving of time and careful thought is appreciated.

QUESTIONS

1. How's Sally doing?
   (If parent remarks, "You are the one to know that," reply that a teacher can never be as close to a child as her parent or know as well how she is doing; the way she is in school is only half the picture or much less than half.)

2. What do you think right now are Sally's worst faults and habits which maybe we don't see at school?
   (This is deliberately so worded to allow parent to show resentment of child if he has hostile feelings.)

3. What are some of her best qualities and habits which we may only partly see at school?
   (Questions 2 and 3 are planned to allow the parent to reveal negative and positive attitudes freely. Get parent to be specific—give specific behavior incidents so that remarks can be compared. If necessary, say "Would you explain?")

4. What are the kinds of things you don't let or don't want your children to do?
   (If parent says, "I can't think of anything in particular," say, "Can you think of anything you'd prefer her not to do?")

5. How do you try to select your child's playmates?
   (The question is so worded in order to permit the parent who does impose his ideas on his child to feel free to say so. Get parent to be specific.)

6. What would you like the school to do for Sally?
   (Get parent to be as specific as possible.)

7. You know this neighborhood better than I do; are there opportunities you would like your child to have which she doesn't have?

8. From the standpoint of taking care of your family, how do you find your living arrangements? What's good or bad about them?
   (Give this question in an offhand manner, assuming that whatever the home setup is, the parent will have some ideas to offer.)

9. How would you change things for your child if you could?
   a) at home?
   b) at school?
   c) just in general—in the neighborhood or in this town generally?

(The entire question should be read as a whole first, and then go back to *a, b,* and *c* for separate responses. If parent says, "In no way," in regard to "at home," accept this response and go on to "and at school?" etc.)

10. What are your hopes for Sally? What are your husband's hopes? (Give both these questions in one sentence, and then say, "Will you give me yours first and then your husband's?" This question is so worded in order to permit the parent to state easily difference in opinion between the two parents.)

11. Are there courses or experiences which you wish the school offered your child which are not offered at present? For instance, what things interest your child which the school is not teaching? Does she show this interest at home?

12. How do you think Sally's health is at present? How is her appetite? Does she eat as much or as many kinds of food as you would wish? (Try to secure typical day's diet for Sally. If parent says just, "Quite all right," follow with, "Do you remember what foods she ate yesterday or today?")

13. Does Sally lack anything which you think is essential for her or that she should have?

14. What general suggestions would you care to make to the school for Sally's program there? (This is a "closing" question intended to give the parent opportunity to say anything else he may still have on his mind and also to leave him the assurance that the school wants to do everything it can for the child's welfare.)

What can be learned from such home interviews can be illustrated by comparing two interviews in contrasting home settings with mothers of two sixth-grade boys in the same classroom. In the one case, the child, Wilbur, was found to be restricted in his social contacts and in any decisions he could make. He was constantly supervised and made to "mind if he gets unruly" on any score from "fighting" to being "saucy." The mother said, "I don't know what my hopes are. He's gonna go to work. Gonna get him a job." As to the father's opinions, "He didn't say anything yet." The mother comments, "Wilbur never says what he likes best," and "He's always glad when Monday comes." His "nice manners" and "minding" at home formed a part of a fairly passive picture of interaction with his parents. Wilbur's mother said, "He's doing fine in writing and arithmetic."

The other boy, David, was given freedom of decision extending from whomever he cared to associate with to what future he might plan for himself. David's mother pictures him as liking people, "He will ask anybody anything he wants to know, no matter who they are." In regard to friends, "We let them [David and his brother] pick them." The boy was expected to make up his own mind, and "I can trust and I do depend on him." He lived in an atmosphere in which, according to his mother, "We never forbid them—we tell them if it's wrong to do something, they take our word." The mother admired David for not letting other white children influence him against Negro people. "When they say, 'There are no good ones,' " she said he answers, " 'There are,' " and " 'in my class, too.' " She approved of his making friends with them. As to hopes for him, she wanted "him to be what he wants to be," and "Of course, if it's what he wants to do, he'll be good at it." She added that she'd like him to go to college. The mother said the school "is doing a pretty good job. He's learning, and he's learning to get along with other people."

The first boy was unchosen in school, while the second was much chosen. This relationship between sociometric position and home position was usually found. Children who are most deprived of affection from school-fellows are similarly least privileged in their home settings on many counts. Children who are frequently chosen in school are likewise found to enjoy a good deal of affection, respect, and confidence at home. Often even the concepts and skills children show in school can be traced to the fostering of certain outlooks and ways of behavior at home. Home interviews in general help to uncover points at which children are stopped in their growth toward understanding and skills in human relations, or learn ways of conduct which run counter to what is expected of them in school.

SUCCESSIVE SOCIOGRAMS AND TIME INTERVALS

Follow-up sociograms are naturally most useful for checking on growth after some action has been taken on the basis of the first one. If children have been reseated, committees rearranged, or some teaching and guidance toward understanding human relations undertaken, it is interesting to study any results in another sociometric test.

Much has been said in passing of the importance of more than one sociogram in assessing a social situation. Sociograms portraying many classes or a whole school on the same day will supplement and correct one another to some extent. They will also serve to point up any major persistent conditions in the school regulations or the local community which may be seriously affecting group life. Any minor or purely transitory influences in a single classroom will be seen in proper perspective through the combined impact of the series, and significant influences will be highlighted. For motivating these new choices, some rearrangement or new classification can be asked for as soon as the original committees have finished their work, or new projects come up, or new experiments are to be tried.

But most important, the use of successive sociograms gives individuals continuing opportunity to exercise choice and to learn to act in their own behalf and to live by their decisions. For relationships to be well explored and enjoyed, time is essential. Yet a fixed arrangement that continues over the school year allows the group to become stagnant—lacking in stimulation—a situation as unfortunate as quickly altering periods that do not allow sufficient time for relationships to mature.

Any second or additional sociometric test should be given after a time interval long enough to make sense to the group members —to justify it from their point of view. Thus, the time interval must be long enough to register a considerable degree of change in the structure. For children in classes up to the third grade, four or five weeks is sufficient for this purpose; for fourth, fifth, and sixth grades, six weeks is about adequate; from the seventh grade on, at least seven and preferably eight weeks should be allowed. There are, of course, situations where particular projects call for a shorter or much longer time duration of the choice structure. However, the principles applying are the same: the sociometric test should primarily meet the felt needs of the members, and only when it does so are the data valid for research purposes.

The importance of *different criteria* to the results in sociometric testing is very clear.[10] If exact comparison is essential, the test situation should not be altered. Thus, if seating was the situation in the first one, the same criterion should be used also in the second

---

[10] See especially chap. v.

one. However, for a general study of association patterns such as the prevailing social atmosphere or the degree of integration, a change in the test situation can be helpful.

A series of sociograms of a single group will provide many correctives for interpretation. The really decisive factors and key individuals are emphasized. Transitory influences, such as the effect of coming together again after the summer vacation or assimilating newcomers, will be recorded on a diminishing scale, and the persisting factors will begin to stand out. The effects of changes in the school arrangements or curriculum will be reflected and can, accordingly, be appraised.

In order to compare successive sociograms, each new sociogram must be analyzed in approximately the same manner as was the initial one, and the resulting interpretations should then be compared. For most purposes a rough check on such aspects as shifts in the pattern of choice or rejection, in the number of highly chosen and unchosen individuals, in the formation of cliques and the like, will be sufficient. Those desiring to conduct a more careful study may be aided by the schedule which follows.

SOCIOMETRIC WORK SCHEDULE

COMPARATIVE ANALYSIS OF TWO SUCCESSIVE SOCIOGRAMS

If answer to any question is "yes," give your opinion in regard to possible causes.

1. Are there any major alterations in the structure, reflecting shifts on the part of a large portion of the members?
2. Are there certain major consistencies?
3. Do any new mutual structures appear?
4. Do any new unchosen structures appear?
5. What unchosen structures, if any, found on the first sociogram are not found on this sociogram?
6. Have any mutual choice structures become mutual rejections?
7. Have any mutual rejection structures become mutual choices?
8. Have any cleavages among groups found on the first sociogram become modified or extended?
   boy-girl
   economic
   national backgrounds
   religious
   home situation
   academic ability

being employed after school
prestige of some group factor
other group factor
9. Have choices developed or fallen off between some much-chosen individuals and other much-chosen individuals?
10. How does the proportion of amount of choices to amount of rejections compare on the two sociograms?
11. How do the directions of expression of rejection compare on the two sociograms?
12. Viewing the two structures as "wholes," how does this sociogram compare with the first in respect to indications of group integration, such as disappearance of closed cliques, wider distribution of much-chosen individuals?
13. Do you see anything in this sociogram which may indicate that certain individuals are developing new needs which were not evident on the first sociogram?

Shifts in the relative prominence of specific individuals are frequently found when the problem of group relations has been seriously treated in class; some of those originally considered important may not stand up under the standards that may have developed. Usually such changes are the outgrowth of some new social arrangement or some new concepts according to which pupils now appraise one another. For example, in one instance, "that crowd," at first rejected as being "snobs," was later accepted when their classmates came to understand that its members "were really waiting to be approached just as we had been waiting for them to approach us."

Whatever significant changes may have been found, however, the chief value of successive sociograms lies in their emphasis on the degree of stability within the structure as a whole and on the relative slowness with which members alter the feelings they have about one another. While different criteria show different results, whenever the same criterion is employed at different times, the results reveal that shifts in feeling between individuals are not rapid—even among nursery and prenursery children.

Often from an observer's vantage point, interpersonal feelings appear to be in great flux. The sociometric evidence is that the individual's observed behavior is not a reliable index to what associates he wants; too many factors beyond his control may affect his behavior.

III. USES AND APPLICATIONS

SOCIOMETRIC DATA CAN BE USED IN LEARNING SITUATIONS IN MANY ways, for the composition of groups has a bearing on the quality of personal relations in almost everything that happens in school. Individual schools obviously have different problems in this respect, since they carry on their work under different conditions and with student bodies that vary in size and personal characteristics. As a result, sociograms have been put to a wide range of uses, as a few brief examples, which follow, illustrate.

CARRYING OUT THE ORIGINAL AGREEMENT

The immediate thing to do about the findings of a sociometric test is to carry out the agreement made with the children when they were asked to indicate their choices. The class must be reseated as soon as possible, or the committees appointed, or the plans made for the party or the school trip, or whatever it was. This is the teacher's first real opportunity to prove to the children that she considers their preferences important. The principle for translating sociometric data into action is simple and the same for all purposes: each individual should be given the highest degree of satisfaction compatible with maximum happiness for everyone else and maximum stimulation for all. In other words, the object is to provide for each child the best possible arrangement from *his* point of view, but since the same consideration must be shown to all of his classmates, there will have to be some compromise. The following rules have justified themselves in practice.

First, in order to carry out as many expressed wishes as possible, it is generally best to start with the children who have not been chosen at all or only seldom. It is usually advisable to give an unchosen pupil his own first choice. For example, if David chooses

Patty first, Lee second, and Willard third, and no one chooses him —then David should be placed with Patty.

Second, give any pupil in a pair relation the highest reciprocated choice from *his* point of view: his first choice if this is returned, his second if this is returned and his first is not, or his third if this is the only reciprocated choice on his list. For example, if Patty chooses Lynne first, Susan second, and Robert third, but neither Susan nor Robert returns the choice; and if Lynne has chosen Patty second while her first and third choices have not been reciprocated, then both Patty and Lynne will have received optimal treatment if they are put together.

Third, if a child has received choices only from people other than the ones he chose, then give him his first choice. Suppose Paul chooses Edward, Gordon, and Tony in that order, but is chosen by three quite different classmates; the best placement for Paul is with Edward. Fourth, if there have been any rejections, make sure that no such unchosen child is put with those boys and girls who have asked not to be with him. Fifth and last, check the final arrangement to make sure that every child has been placed with at least one of his indicated choices.

Exception to the above principles of placement is made whenever the sociometric results are such that, in carrying out the principles, cleavages appearing in the sociometric patterns would become apparent to the members of the group through the placement itself. Under these circumstances, the group factors take precedence, and a lower degree of choice is used.

For example, if boys and girls are found to choose from their own sex almost exclusively, the placement should carry out all the boy-girl choices that were made; such choices may, for example, be second or third choices. At the same time boys and girls should be so scattered about in the seating arrangement of the homeroom, or in the formation of committees—whatever the sociometric question specified—that neither group can surmise that there were few choices between them.

Thus, the condition of confidentiality of choices is kept.

Group factors to which the teacher should be alert differ from group to group; among the most usual are: religion, race, nationality background, socioeconomic level, separate transportation to school, after-school or other work, newcomer and old resident.

But the group factor principle in sociometric placement has other reasons than confidentiality to support it. Sociometric placement aims both at fulfilling and expanding the individual's interpersonal experience. Diffidence, lack of experience, and doubt as to reception can often create or maintain factions; careful sociometric placement can prevent such inhibiting factors from becoming attributes of group factors. When through placement a pupil's interpersonal understanding and experience are fostered, he is, to that extent, encouraged to reach out more readily; thus a step is taken to forestall prejudice from developing, increasing, or continuing.

Occasionally the configuration of choices is such that it is impossible to accommodate everyone with one of his choices in the arrangement. Though this rarely happens, it is important that the technique used in meeting the situation be honest and direct. The experiences of numerous teachers demonstrate that it is the much-chosen pupil—whether child or older student—who is most ready to accept the bad news that, the way the jigsaw puzzle of choices came out, he cannot be given any one of his choices without depriving several other students of theirs. He can be called aside and told the simple truth: so many whom he did not choose want to be with him that it is necessary to ask him to accept an arrangement that gives others what they want while, for the time being, he foregoes his own choices, which may have been reciprocated. At the same time he should be assured that when the next occasion for choosing takes place, if anyone must be asked to make an adjustment, it will not be he. In some score of years of this writer's experience with teachers in this country and elsewhere, there has been no instance in which the much-chosen, when so approached, did not willingly rise to the occasion. Their reaction is one of adventure and surprise and good cheer at the idea that they could be wanted from unexpected quarters.

It becomes obvious to any teacher why this strategy is psychologically sound: much-chosen individuals do not find interrelating to others the kind of problem which average-chosen and under-chosen individuals do; in general, they find great satisfaction in giving of themselves, which is, of course, in part why they are so much chosen. It is equally obvious to any teacher, as she comes to know the poignant needs of children who are consistently unchosen or underchosen, why it is not desirable from a mental hygiene point of view to ask of them postponement of interpersonal fulfillment.

Most teachers notice an immediate effect on their students when they have carried out original agreements in ways outlined above. In many cases, tensions that were due to blocked communication or feelings of not belonging were eliminated. How this happens is illustrated by an anecdote in a primary school. Charles had been uncommunicative and apparently disinterested in his surroundings. On a sociometric test he was unchosen, and the child he had named first was Michael, the most-asked-for boy in the class. When the new seating was announced, Charles found that he had been placed with his first choice. He smiled broadly, rushed to Michael, and stretched out his hand to him saying, "I am happy to be by you, Michael!" The other child rose to the occasion and said, "That's swell, I'll say!" as he proceeded to help Charles with his things. In this instance, the two-way benefit of sociometric placement is to be noted. The overchosen boy had perhaps not known that Charles cared so much for him; he only knew, for his part, that he had neither chosen nor rejected Charles. In the new security given to Charles by Michael, the former's attitude toward schoolwork could be influenced by the specific desire to show Michael that he could do the work after all. An individual whose opinion he valued was now a reality in his interpersonal world. But the most significant result was that the opinion Charles held of himself could take a more constructive turn.

It must be pointed out, however, that the effects of reseating or any other rearrangement may not always be immediately apparent. Sometimes the first results may even seem negative. For example, one teacher reported that reseating resulted in increased noise and talk, whispering, and other annoying behavior. This lasted twelve days. Then the boys and girls settled down to their new freedom. Committees based on expressed choices often seem to spend all their time at first enjoying one another, but eventually they get busy and then produce better work than formerly. The simple fact is that time is needed for girls and boys to adjust to the new situation. Among the many teachers who have used sociometric choices and continued their arrangements over a period of time, none have reported more than temporary disturbances, and all have found that their classroom atmosphere and working morale have increased markedly. Only at the start do children require especial patience while they learn new skills and accommodate themselves to new methods, especially if these represent radical departures from what they have been used to.

ASSISTING INDIVIDUAL CHILDREN

One of the chief aims in improving human relationships is to help individuals to find both personal security and appropriate roles in groups. If social arrangements are to accomplish this purpose, it is of the utmost importance to work with and through each child's feelings and standards rather than against them. This applies to all matters, from selecting pupils for positions of control over the others to singling out individuals for praise or comment. The consequence of disregarding the students' values may be illustrated by the case of Joan in a girls vocational high school. She was a bright and industrious student and had often been picked out for a commendation by the faculty. The sociogram indicated that Joan was definitely not wanted by her classmates as a work associate. The teachers, thinking that they might have been responsible for this situation, decided not to pay her any exceptional attention. Apparently this helped matters for, when another sociometric test was given some eight weeks later, only one girl in the class indicated that she did not want to serve on the same committee as Joan. In this case, the faculty had unknowingly been contributing to her rejection.

In an elementary school, Miss L was surprised to find from her sociometric analysis that Sally's choices had not been reciprocated although the child had seemed to have friends. True, one of the other girls in the room was always with Sally, but they lived in the same block. From informal talks with the other children, Miss L discovered that Sally was thought of as "not playing fair," as "too bossy," and as "too fat." Further observation indicated that Sally was not "in" things very much, that she stood around on the edges to watch, as if hoping to be asked to join, that she brought books from home to share with the others, and that she offered to help on occasions, only to be turned down. Miss L decided to make use of Catherine, one of the class leaders, to help advance Sally's social position. The opportunity came when the class chose new chairmen for committees. She mentioned to Catherine that Sally might make a good chairman for housekeeping because of the many fine suggestions she had made for the room in the past and because of her generosity with her books.

Catherine agreed and actually nominated Sally at the appropriate time. Sally was elected and showed her pleasure with a "big smile" in Catherine's direction. That afternoon something was planned that called for more books than there were to go round; the children were asked to sit with whomever they wished to look on with. Miss L was interested to "see Sally go immediately to sit with her new friend," while Catherine "received her graciously, smiling and making room for her right away." After that, Sally was able to take her part in group activities happily and was increasingly accepted by the others. It was the sociogram that gave Miss L the first clue both to Sally's difficulty and to Catherine's strategic position to help her.

When pupils are widely unwanted by their classmates—not simply ignored—the problem is frequently more complex. The two most actively rejected children in a particular eighth grade, for instance, were both discovered to be very unhappy at home. Both were only children. One of them was a ward of the state placed out with grandparents who were not sympathetic. The other was living with a widowed mother who was severe and repressive with the child; the mother also seemed to be ambitious for her daughter beyond the child's seeming ability. Real attack on such conditions can obviously be made only through the joint efforts of social workers and school personnel. At the same time, individual teachers can and do help matters at least for the period spent in the classroom. In the above eighth grade, for instance, following the administration of the first sociogram, discussion and instruction were focused on helping boys and girls appreciate human problems and personal difficulties. As a result, on two subsequent sociograms the number of rejections each of the girls received decreased markedly.[1]

Often sociograms suggest ways of preventing rejection from crystallizing around a particular child or a set of children. One teacher's account illustrates this.

Maxwell was one of my rejects—and his school history shows he had always been a "fringer"—not liked by the children, troublesome, and a tattletale. He is fat, awkward, and possesses a below-average mentality. One would probably soon have become aware of his aloneness without the sociogram—but through individual conferences following the sociometric tests, I learned reasons for his rejection by the children, which might have otherwise never become known to me. He didn't do anything very well, he tattled on the kids, he was fat, and he had smelly feet. To get a boy like that into a group can become something of a problem. I had two fortunate experiences with him.

One day I saw him on the playground with a shiny new football and with a crowd of boys around him. Because of the extremely small size of our playgrounds, it has been necessary to ban balls. So when the boys saw me in the window, they scattered like flies and left Maxwell, alone, holding the ball and caught in the act of breaking a building rule. When they came in, I admired the ball, and said it was too bad we couldn't make some use of it. Someone suggested using it for gym that day, a suggestion hailed with joy by the class. Maxwell was elected umpire for the day, a special honor, usually bestowed on only the best. And the class learned, that day, that Maxwell could be a very fair and capable umpire, instead of the awkward slow-moving athlete they had formerly known him to be.

I had tried to get various of the popular boys to play with him after school, but as no one lived nearby, I had little success. So I finally contacted his mother and told her we had a new boy who found it difficult to make friends and wondered if she would have Maxwell have him in, perhaps for lunch or for play after school. Never dreaming it was her son who was being doctored, she fell in with the plan most enthusiastically, and a fair friendship has developed between the two boys, which sometimes includes one or two others.

Whatever success has attended such efforts as those here described, of course, reflects the degree to which the psychological problem was correctly appraised as well as the appropriateness of

---

[1] See Hilda Taba *et al., Literature for Human Understanding,* and Margaret M. Heaton and Helen B. Lewis, *Reading Ladders for Human Relations* (Rev. ed.; Washington: American Council on Education, 1955) for suggestions and description of well-developed techniques of such discussion.

the action taken. Teachers are successful in numerous instances; the sociometric material is often enough to guide the insight they have already developed through classroom experience.

RESHAPING GENERAL PRACTICES

In most schools there are administrative routines and regulations which often affect the normal development of social interaction in ways that had not been anticipated. Sociometric studies frequently point up the consequences and thus provide a realistic basis for reconsidering the practices which may have caused them. For example, in a certain elementary school, sociometric tests were given simultaneously to the entire student body. The results indicated that, beginning in the third grade and increasing sharply after that, there was a cleavage between boys and girls significantly exceeding what is usually found. When the teachers tried to account for this situation, they first fell back upon explanations about growing up, self-consciousness, and the prevalence of teasing. Then they began to wonder if the school arrangements were emphasizing the division and experimented by changing the recess rules. Hitherto boys and girls had been sent to opposite ends of the playground with the understanding that they were not to mix. The idea had been to avoid their quarreling. Next, the teachers arranged mixed squads of boys and girls in the gym so that a new organization for games came into being which could be easily transferred to the playground. The earlier decided competition between girl and boy squads was seen to disappear. The third change had to do with mixed traffic patrols, each team consisting of equal numbers of boys and girls.

Results began to show in a very short time. After only a few weeks the teachers reported "a freer interchange on the playground," "a more helpful relation between girls and boys" in the gym, and that the patrols worked "more smoothly." Furthermore, there was less teasing in the classrooms, girls and boys did things together more and more naturally, and there was "no longer any giggling or sly glances" when Mary sat down to help John with some problem. Some of the parents commented on the "nice relationship" between the girls and boys at parties. Additional sociometric tests made later showed substantial increases in the number of mutual choices throughout, as well as in choices between boys and girls, and likewise indicated that the number of unchosen individuals had been reduced markedly. These changes took place within less than an academic year.

In another elementary school, sociograms throughout showed that the structure of the several classes appeared from two to four years below the stage of development normally reached by children of the same ages. In talks with the pupils about why they had chosen as they did, a very common answer was: "They are just the ones I know." Many children explained their failure to write down three names by saying, "I don't know other people." This situation led the faculty to reconsider the rule against conversation in the halls, to institute a daily period of free talk in the home-rooms, and to get the children to work out, with their teachers, projects for activity programs which they could share in carrying out. The development of social skills was placed among the major objectives of the school curriculum.

A high school had a problem in the cafeteria: boys and girls grouped themselves separately, and the noise amounted to a din. The faculty wanted to make conditions more livable for all and were particularly interested in improving relations between boys and girls. They had already used sociograms for seating in home-rooms. On the basis of the results, a boy and girl who were highly chosen were invited to act as host and hostess at each table. These individuals, it was assumed, would break the tradition of staying on separate sides of the cafeteria, since the pupils who had chosen them would follow suit in order to sit with them. In this instance, the teachers were building on the influence of much-wanted associates to broaden concepts of acceptable behavior and help the group as a whole to outgrow its conventions.

Other regulations that have been found to have similarly retarding effects on natural association include marching in pairs to the auditorium, entering and leaving school in the same way two by two, seating boys and girls on opposite sides of the classroom, dismissing students in groups according to sex, and the like. Any other form of segregation shows repercussions in kind; it commonly has the result of building up several social sets within the student body as a whole.

A grade-wide regrouping of students in the homeroom, using sociometric choices as a basis, but also distributing the variety of capacities and of leadership positions in all groups, is found to be one way to ameliorate the consequences of ability grouping. In such a two-way arrangement the range of academic ability, and of the capacity to relate oneself to others is present in each group, and thus the heterogeneity of the whole student body is represented in each group. A high school with an extremely low student morale regrouped its freshmen and sophomores in homerooms in the foregoing manner. This improved student attitudes and application to schoolwork to such an extent that later the eleventh and twelfth grades were also regrouped. Teachers' reactions were contrary to those usually expected in regard to teaching heterogeneous groups: "It is more fun to teach this year, we have more interested pupils; at least, *I* have better classes than I did," "We are getting a better grade of student this year." Actually, the school population was unchanged, but the child leadership had been distributed, and the network of affinities had been realigned. Procedure of this sort is especially important in schools where students, because of the meagerness of their outside lives, must get whatever satisfactions they can from human relations almost entirely in school.

Similar methods were used in an elementary school where pupils were organized in "opportunity" groups for slow learners and "regular" groups for other students. One teacher who had students from both groups in her homeroom tried to engage them in activities together. When she asked for sociometric choices in connection with certain proposed committees, it appeared that all of the opportunity students wanted to be with the regular ones, but that they were either ignored or rejected by the latter. The teacher carefully arranged her activity groups so as to give each one some of his chosen companions and, at the same time, to put children of both classifications together in varying proportions. The work proceeded smoothly for several weeks until the project was completed. When the teacher then asked how they had liked the committee procedure, the pupils were so enthusiastic that new committees were at once set up for the balance of the semester. Every member of the class approved of the method whereby assignments had been made. In this instance, long-standing prejudice and unpleasant tension were being broken down through new opportunity for pupils to know one another in work relationships.

GROUPING FOR WORK

Most schools use informal arrangements for work such as committees, panels, or special-interest groups. As teachers saw that performance in such working groups was closely related to their interpersonal structure, they began using the sociometric choices as one factor in composing these groups. In such work groups, it is important not only to fulfill a pupil's choices in order to release his energies, but also to provide for a balance of skills and significant mutual stimulation.

In setting up the working groups, the following suggestions will be helpful:

First, vary the size of the committee according to how easily students enter into interrelations. The more difficult this is for them, the smaller the size of the group should be. To permit full leeway in carrying out the arrangement, size should not be stated in advance.

Second, in groups which are closed formations, include other students; or detach two or more students (so that the relatedness is not completely broken) and add others to them. The purpose is to prevent the students in closed cliques from continuing to be conspicuously off by themselves and to give them a chance to relate themselves to other students.

Third, vary the composition of each committee so as to make it a heterogeneous mixture of such differences as sex, age levels, home backgrounds, and ability. The aim is to provide as varied as possible experience in association.

Fourth, whenever a mixed group of students are to work together for the first time, include more than one individual for each difference in order to minimize possible self-consciousness. For example, if boys and girls have not worked together before, include at least two or three girls on any committee largely composed of boys. This applies to every group factor that matters, such as place of residence, race, religion.

Fifth, divide up the unchosen students so that not more than two at the most will be in each working group of six or more, and give each the most advantageous interpersonal surroundings that the total situation permits. What this means in terms of group structure, then, is that there should always be a few highly chosen students and roughly the same number of unchosen individuals on each committee, and that there should be at least as many students of average sociometric position as of the other two types combined. The same procedure holds for any type of working group—panels for book discussions, project committees, discussion groups, and the like.

Obviously, there is nothing arbitrary about these principles, nor should anyone expect to apply these principles with maximum effectiveness at the first trial. But many teachers have discovered in themselves, as they have experimented with the procedure, a growing proficiency in the art of estimating what will promote the development of their pupils, what each is ready for, how their several temperaments will balance and supplement one another, and how the particular skills of each will interact and find expression in the task at hand.

A simple illustration of temperamental considerations may be cited. Irene's class had had little previous experience in working in small groups. When the idea was proposed of trying out the committee system, she ranked among the top twenty percent on the score of choices received in this connection. In class discussion Irene had always been able to hold her own—perhaps rather more than her own. Her teacher, Miss F, decided to put Irene with other girls all of whom had chosen her, but to use only one of the three mutual choices she had received. Miss F did this quite deliberately in the hope that Irene would be elected chairman; she was. In her new role, Irene had the learning experience of getting others to talk and exchange ideas; before this development she had been observed to listen to her classmates hardly at all except in social situations. As time went on, Irene came to enjoy the function of getting lively discussion from her committee, and she transferred this new skill increasingly to the general discussion periods in class.

Miss F had foreseen that if Irene had been placed with all three of her mutual friends, she might have earned for herself the resentment or rejection of her other classmates, for all three of the girls in question might have let her steal the show from whatever chairman had been elected. When she met a real challenge—under congenial circumstances—to her tendency to monopolize the floor, she was able to learn a new skill.

Miss F would probably not have been successful with Irene if she had put the girl with many other students of equal ability. Several of fairly different abilities will be helpful whenever the object is to accommodate outstanding individuals or to display special abilities prominently. This situation arises, for instance, when a teacher wants to let the class get to know and appreciate some talent they may not have suspected, or when an able but shy girl or boy needs a little success by way of encouragement, or, again, when there are gifted students in the group whose special contributions should be valuable to all. In this event, then, one needs to keep in mind that each student of unusual ability needs lots of social space in which to function. It is, therefore, usually desirable not to have more than one or two such individuals in the same working group and to see that there are roughly twice as many students less capable for the task. As far as the latter are concerned, the competition should never be so great as to discourage them and make them give up altogether. If the girls and boys actually supplement one another on the score of special aptitudes, the situation is usually educative.

GROUPING FOR CLUBS

So far most of the discussion has had to do with examples from classroom procedure. Sociograms have been used just as effectively, however, in connection with extracurricular activities and various aspects of group living. The identical principles come into play in these instances as in the classroom situations. It will, accordingly, be useful here only to show their application in a variety of cases.

One of these examples is set in a large high school with a cosmopolitan population. The ethnic strains most frequently represented among the students were Italian and other southern European.

The faculty was concerned about the number of fights in and around school and tended to attribute them to antagonism between Italians and other southeastern Europeans. Clubs had been abolished a few years before because of "their bad morale." The staff thought the time had come to introduce them again under conditions that would ensure pleasant relations. The possibility of using sociometric choices was suggested, and attention was called to the fact that sociometric data might throw light on the cause of the cleavages. Students from three grade levels were asked to name the three individuals with whom they would prefer to be associated in a club. The sociometric question included the following statement, prepared by the principal and read simultaneously in each homeroom:

Sometimes schools begin clubs by announcing which clubs are available and asking who wants to join each one of them. This is one way to form clubs so that those interested in doing the same thing can have the opportunity to be together. But then you don't know who will be in that club with you, and often you may want to be in the same club with certain other boys and girls whom you enjoy being with. It is much harder to arrange membership this way as it has to be done way ahead of time. So we will take a few minutes now to ask you to make your choices. . . . Think of everyone you know, but don't talk now; make the choices your own.

The resulting data showed up no marked cleavage along ethnic lines, but rather pointed to a remarkable paucity of social pattern: there were hardly any networks of association, certain students were clustered in self-contained little groups, and many girls and boys had not been chosen at all. The problem of the faculty, therefore, was to set up the clubs so that each would have several highly chosen individuals to focus interest and morale, and to distribute the unchosen students so that they would have a chance to function and become acquainted. Information supplied by interest questionnaires, filled out at the time the sociometric test was administered, was useful in placing these girls and boys where they would find opportunity to be active and to participate.

The next example illustrates how sociometric methods may be combined with other diagnostic devices for maximum usefulness. The setting is another large high school situated, this time, in a well-to-do suburban residential section of a medium-sized city.

There was religious cleavage in the neighborhood as well as in the school between the dominant Lutherans and, more especially, the Jews, though also the Roman Catholics. Even more acute was the resentment over sorority membership; there were ten sororities in the school with a combined membership of approximately four hundred out of seventeen hundred students. And yet, there was no correspondingly bitter antagonism over fraternities; there were only three of them, and they did not enjoy the prestige either of the Hi-Y clubs or of the sororities. The unhappiness and frustration of many of the girls were shared by their mothers; there was criticism from some parents of the social opportunities provided in school. The faculty disapproved of the sororities very much and was likewise disturbed by the religious division.

During the first year many preliminary inquiries were made largely on the basis of interviews with parents, students, and members of the faculty. The evidence pointed to considerable unhappiness and exasperation among all, including the sorority members —but nobody had any idea of what to do. The investigation seemed to be generating more heat than light and thus aggravating matters. During the following year one of the teachers of the tenth grade hit upon the expedient of discussing the problems of newcomers in any environment. She read with her students a series of stories on the feelings, aspirations, and adjustment problems of immigrants to America from a variety of backgrounds. In this connection the discussion was guided over into speculation about the similar feelings that newcomers to the school might be experiencing. Other teachers and students were interested in this approach. It was suggested by the Intergroup Education project staff that a general survey of student participation in activities of the school might yield something tangible on which to base future policy.

At the end of the year, therefore, when the freshmen had been in school some six months, a check was taken of their club membership and active interests in school affairs. A participation check list was distributed in the homerooms and a sociometric question was added: the boys and girls were asked to indicate in order of preference the three students they would most want to be with if new clubs were organized in the near future. This combination instrument was filled out in all but two of the tenth-grade homerooms, and returns were collected from approximately three hundred and fifty tenth-grade students.

The findings were significant in helping define the problem further. More than two-thirds of the boys and one-fifth of the girls belonged to no school clubs at all. Both sexes seemed to be most interested in clubs that were neither academic nor athletic in focus, but the social clubs had never included both sexes. Since the most popular and esteemed boys clubs—the Hi-Y organizations—were small in membership (varying from sixteen to twenty-two), they were not in a position to invite the sororities (of around forty members each) to their parties or dances. Only the academic clubs encouraged both girls and boys to join. As a result, there were few opportunities for boys and girls to meet outside the classroom unless they did so by individual invitation in each other's homes. Furthermore, many students did not actually know what the activity program of the school already offered; they suggested interest clubs already available.

The sociometric data added another important slant to the picture. While a few students received unusually large numbers of choices—fourteen, twenty-two, and even thirty-two were the highest scores—an exceptionally high percentage received either only one choice or none at all. Moreover, twice as many boys as girls were unchosen. A large number of students, considerably more boys than girls, were thus in the position of apparently not being known or sought after by their classmates. The girls more often than the boys seemed to be in an untenable psychological position of conflict in social relationship; more than six times as many girls as boys were in the difficult position of receiving choices only from classmates whom they had not chosen themselves. There were very few cross-sex choices, and this is not the usual pattern for tenth grades. Altogether, the findings indicated that these young people were in need of help from the school in matters of social development.

A few quotations from statements made by students in a series of confidential interviews on the school's social life illustrate student views of their predicament. The quotations have been selected to show something of the students' own analyses and also of their attitudes and feelings on the subject:

For me I think it's been easy [to make friends]; the people are so nice, the kids are so easy to talk to. It's hard for some people, though. . . . A lot don't try to help new girls who come to the school, and that's where a lot of us are wrong sometimes. The *real* clubs here you have to be asked into, and so you'd have to make your friends before you went into one of those. You get rushed into them. Then it's easy for her from then on. . . the outside clubs I mean. We consider what she could do for the club, have her to tea, call back in a week if we want her. If she made friends with girls who are in clubs, she might be invited, but it's hard for a new girl, they'd think she's different if she's a new girl and so it isn't sure. . . . When you're from a different place you don't know the ways, like dressing. The kids who don't belong usually go around with other kids who aren't in. . . . But those who don't dress like us I haven't got to know so well, so I don't know what they're like—it keeps you apart. [A sorority girl.]

When I first came it was hard to get acquainted, and they have their own groups, and it's sort of hard to get into. I wouldn't join a club [sorority] because I don't believe in them. . . . I said I didn't really want to join—I never was asked, maybe because I spoke what I meant. [A nonsorority girl.]

In this school it's just you have to grow up with the soil. . . . I find it easy, but if you're from another place, it's not easy at all because the school is divided into a lot of little groups and it's next to impossible for someone from somewhere else to enjoy themselves here. I know if I was new here, I'd be friendly with people and still they wouldn't be to me. I belong to . . . , and if I hadn't gotten into any club at all it would have meant a lot to me that I didn't. If I hadn't been asked, it definitely would have left a mark on me. I'd probably gotten a complex, I don't know what kind, and feel I was inferior to people. [A sorority girl.]

In a sorority you're sure of having friends there, but the outsiders have a grudge against you. Some don't believe in it. I don't know about what I'd do if I were asked into one; you're not anybody unless you have cashmere as well as angora [sweaters]. Girls have it harder than boys because boys don't choose by such superficial things as how much money they have, and boys have a better chance to mix in athletics. . . . [A nonsorority girl.]

When you go with any girl not in a sorority, you're not talked about so much, and the girl's not discouraged at the boy. After you date a sorority girl, the others try to discourage her about you and they can say anything they think of, and the girl can't make up her own mind about you. When you like her you're supposed to put up with all of them, too! [A boy.]

The sororities make it hard for a lot of kids, and it bothers a lot of my girl friends. My girl friend and I don't belong, and it bothers her not to be able to say she's in one, but not me because my sis was in one and I know it's not missing so much as other kids think. . . . I like to go with all religions, but you get stopped quick and it's hard when you try to do it. I'm Lutheran and a boy's father won't let him take me out; he is Catholic. But it's mostly between Protestants and Jews. . . . Yes, many are hurt because lots of people won't be friends with them, and I heard a girl say: "I wish people wouldn't treat me that way just because I'm Jewish!" They just snubbed her, left her out after school hours, but in school they get everything out of her they can. It isn't right but that's how it is. . . . The sororities tend to break the girl's own standards down, they make her fit the group standard. . . . They come in one mold—you can't tell them separate after they're in. They're alike, that's how I mean—one mold. [A nonsorority girl.]

I think it's too bad that there are girls who don't belong to clubs, and money does make a difference. [A sorority girl.]

The effect of this impersonal factual material was to clear the atmosphere and put the sorority problem in a certain perspective. It was obvious to the faculty and the Parent-Teacher Association that girls and boys needed more opportunities to meet socially, that more individual students ought to be given the chance to become known and to exercise leadership, and that there was room for a much more active and vital program related to the interests of the girls and boys. By the closing months of the academic year, attention had shifted to the constructive steps that could be taken, and discussion veered away from the pros and cons of sorority membership. Parents, students, and teachers were pooling ideas and resources in behalf of the evolving program, and an edition of the school paper was being talked about as a means of acquainting everybody with the range of clubs to be offered. A student committee of sixteen members had been selected, and teachers chosen to act as sponsors, the duties of which were to review "human relations" in the school. A definitive statement of the issue, furnished by the survey and sociograms, as was the case in this instance, usually aids the taking of appropriate practical steps.

ANALYZING CLEAVAGES

Sociometric procedure in group work has many explicit uses. One of these may be taken, for illustration, from a six-year elementary school. A teacher had been asked by several girls what they should do; they wanted to be Girl Scouts but no nearby troop had room for them. A poll of fifth- and sixth-grade girls showed sixty-four candidates. Another teacher with previous scouting experience volunteered to help. The question then became, how to decide who was to be in which troop. In the words of one teacher:

> Since a troop usually divides into three patrols of eight or ten each for discussion, planning, and working purposes, we decided to use a sociogram to find six natural groups—three for each troop. The question we used was: What four girls would you most want in your patrol?
>
> Influencing placement was the need for balancing the number of white and Negro girls in each troop. From the sociogram we made sure that everyone got at least one choice but still gave very conscious consideration to the racial situation. A few girls came in after the first meeting; they were asked to state a single choice and were placed with the person chosen. . . . Holding to choices, we tried to figure the patrols so that neither race would be overwhelmed by the other. It has worked out beautifully.

The accompanying sociogram (see Figure 4) shows the choice patterns from which groupings for patrols were made. It reveals that some members of each race chose members of their own race exclusively. It also shows in the group as a whole a tendency toward separate racial cliques. A possible inference of these findings was that the choice patterns reflected an expectation on the part of members of both races that outside school they would not be allowed to associate as they did in school. Thus the group factor could have carried over into the scout troops, much as it prevailed in the community.

The placement into six patrols may be read from the sociogram—under each name the troop number is designated by a Roman numeral. The sociometric placement used in this instance was built on the premise that the higher the internal morale of a group, the more it can withstand pressure from other groups. This is achieved in several specific ways:

First, in each patrol every girl (but one) receives assignment with someone she had chosen.[2]

Second, insofar as possible, individuals who are much chosen and individuals who are little chosen or unchosen are distributed so that each patrol has as balanced an interpersonal structure as possible.

Third, each patrol is comprised of about an equal number of members of each race, making the biracial situation the usual one. Thus, no member need be self-conscious regarding race in respect to her particular patrol, and none can know that any other members have shown preferences for their own race.

Fourth, and not least, is auspicious timing from the standpoint of intergroup education—at the start of the project, before diffidence between the races can develop or become chronic.

The community setting of the school showed many conflicts between Negro and white persons. The school itself, however, worked constantly and systematically to keep community patterns of feeling from affecting the in-school life of the children. Classroom sociograms at various grade levels made for the purpose of seating arrangements had shown no cleavage between the races. The hope was to prevent tension from arising within the scout troops. The ends served by the skillful work begun by one teacher showed the community the practicability of interracial projects and aided pupils to integrate in-school and out-of-school relationships.

Wherever, as in this instance, cleavages which may be injurious to a group's healthy development are found, first consideration in any educational setting must go to prevention of their perpetuation. As first choices are, under such conditions, apt to go to individuals within the particular subdivision in which choice corresponds to a prejudice that is already taking hold, the use of first choices as the criterion in the sociometric placement would permit the group to see cleavages which otherwise individual

[2] It will be noted that the exception is a girl who has three mutual choices. She might have been placed in Group I or Group II but apparently was asked to enter Group III to balance the size of that group. Such placement should not be made unless the individual is willing to try it after the matter is explained (see p. 50). For example, "The result of the choices shows that several patrols want you. One of these will be the smallest in membership unless you are willing to join it; you were chosen by members of this group whose choices you did not reciprocate."

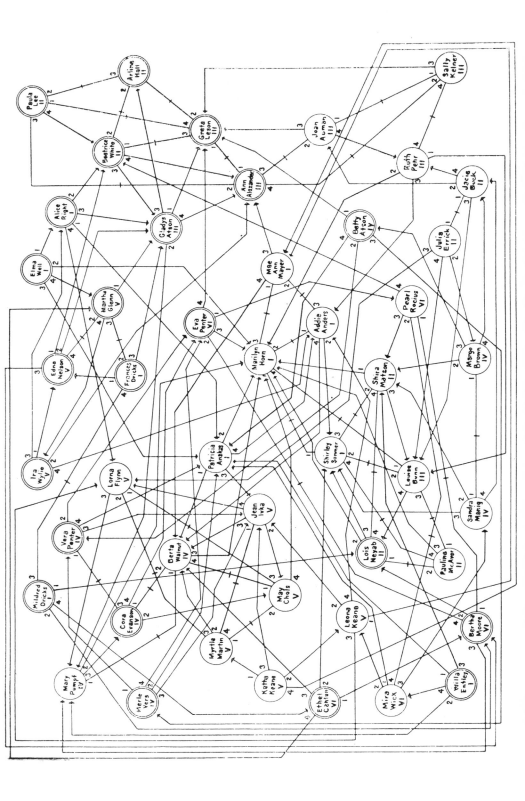

LEGEND ◯ white girl   ◯ Negro girl   ——→ one-way choice   —═— mutual choice   1, 2, 3, or 4 = degree of choice   I, II, III, IV, V, or VI = Group Assigned

Sociometric Question—What four girls would you most want to have in your Patrol?

Sociometric Placement for Membership in Two Troops of 3 Patrols Each from Sociogram for Girl Scouts Patrol

I	II	III	IV
Marilyn Horn	Pauline McAver	Greta Leson N	Berta Walnut
Shirley Sonmer	Lois Neyab N	Ann Alexander N	Mary Pumpf
Addie Anders	Jacie Buck	Sally Kelner	Cora Evanson N
Mae Ann Mayer	Julia Errick	Joan Auman	Vera Penter N
Willa Entley N	Beatrice White N	Ruth Pehr	Betty Atson N
Patricia Anskas	Arline Hall N	Gladys Atson N	Merle Vers N
Alice Right N	Paula Lee N	Louise Bunn	Margo Brown
Elma Well N	Shira Matson	*Dora Atson N	Sandra Manig
Frances Dricks N			*Flora Lespie
Mildred Dricks N			

V	VI
Katha Keane	Mira Wick
Myrtle Martin	Pearl Rocius
May Chols	Bertha Moore N
Jean Ivka	Eva Penter N
Lorna Flynn	*Mammie Tow
Leona Keane	*Lucy Davis N
Martha Glenn N	*Ida Maddon N
Ira Wylie N	Ethel Canton N
Edna Nelson N	*Elaine Harvard N

Note: Influencing placement in patrols was the need for balancing the number of white and Negro girls while giving each person some of her choices. Six girls do not appear on the sociogram. They entered after first meeting. One girl, Louise Bunn, forfeited her choices on request of teacher for sake of others. Two individuals (Mary Pumpf and Arline Hall) gave less than the requested number of choices; this occasionally occurs.

Fig. 4.—Girl Scout sociogram.

members could only guess at. Whenever, instead, second or third choices are used, there is, by the time of the next sociometric test, a considerable reduction of cleavage apparently resulting from increased interpersonal security regarding one's standing in the group as a whole.

Finally, to return to a consideration of sociometric procedure in the classroom, the same principles of placement just described serve in the composition of groups for committee work and the like. A simpler classroom example follows.

For various reasons my classroom was full of sets of pupils—six from a different school, six from a different course which didn't keep them as part of the class most of the day, another bunch who were old acquaintances, ten others whom I continually noticed wandering about from one set to another trying to weave in, several who seemed more sophisticated and who more or less stuck together, and then strayers. I never knew where I was at with so much bidding for my attention.

The sociogram showed me what committee placements to make, and I juggled the choices, making use of those which would cut down the strained relations, and of those which would get students together from the different sets wherever there was a thread between them. I had the class as a whole in mind; so to achieve this, I didn't always use first choices, and I purposely kept committee size open, not saying what size committees would be, so that for the good of all I could vary how many I put together.

From the very start of the choice arrangement I had pleasure in seeing how glad the students were as they worked in their new committees. I put the biggest group of eight in the center spot of the classroom; it had a cross section of almost everything described above. The nucleus set the pace, spreading its initiative, kindling a new interest, and raising morale by working as a team through the chairman they had chosen. Their example was followed by others around them. I am observing the group growing in self-direction, interest, and unity.

There are cleavages other than the kinds recorded above that offer opportunity to benefit group members greatly. The necessity is that each cleavage should be assessed for its effects.

IV. SOCIOMETRIC FINDINGS
SUMMARIZED

SOCIOMETRIC APPROACH INVOLVES USING CHILDREN'S SPONTANEOUS choices as an index for arranging interpersonal relations in the classroom. The soundness of these arrangements, then, depends on the validity of the choices. Two considerations apply in making educational judgments on the basis of sociometric data. One of these is the meaning and the nature of children's choices, because sound educational decisions can be made only if the specific meanings underlying the choices are understood in connection with the patterns revealed in the sociogram.

The second one is the conditions which characterize the association of children at the time of the test. Children choose according to their level of maturity and experience. Freedom to express choices, the maturity of insight into one's own social needs, and the capacity to interact are closely related to the atmosphere which prevails in school. The experience of the Intergroup Education project indicates that in groups where freedom of communication is a rule, when children feel secure in exchanging feelings and ideas, in giving and taking criticism, there is also maturity, clarity, and directedness in their sociometric choices and in their reason for their choices. In other groups where interpersonal communication is repressed, children choose less relevantly and a very few may refrain from choosing altogether. Thus, sociometric evidence from the latter type of group is an index of a lack of social interaction and is only a good clue to how underdeveloped are the specific patterns of association. This chapter will, therefore, be concerned with both the nature of children's choices and the environmental factors that condition their choices, as these were revealed in the work of the cooperating schools. (Further detailed analyses of the major findings are given in chapter v.)

71

THE NATURE OF CHILDREN'S CHOICES

The information on children's choices presented here was derived chiefly from the informal interviews that teachers held with their pupils after the sociometric tests, supplemented or clarified by teachers' reports on their observations and analyses of children's projective themes, such as are described in chapter ii and in research by the writer.[1] The point need hardly be labored that the meaning of and variations in the factors motivating the choices should be understood as fully as possible if educational decisions are to be based upon them.

The usual reasons for choice

Analysis in many public schools of the choices made by children of extremely varied backgrounds indicates that, on the whole, boys and girls tend to enter into association to secure emotional support to function with greater satisfaction in a given context. The specific points at which help is wanted will vary, of course. Often it is a case of personal happiness. Again, it may be understanding well implemented that is wanted, such as is expressed in the following: "He understands me; he understands what my troubles are and what he can do about them," or "He is someone who will share your hardships." Sometimes the choice indicates a direction of the child's sympathy: "She is sweet and helpless; she is sick but keeps her hopes up," or "She tries not to look hurt when someone teases her about her ugliness."

The great majority of choices studied appears to be based on a combination of emotional satisfaction and specific helpfulness which the chooser expects from the individual he has named. Two quotations from statements made in an eighth grade will serve to illustrate.

He helps me a lot in English; he explains things I don't understand. We were close friends in the seventh grade and hit it off swell in the

---

[1] H. H. Jennings, "Sociometric Structure in Personality and Group Formation," in Muzafer Sherif and M. O. Wilson (eds.), *Group Relations at the Crossroads* (New York: Harper & Bros., 1953), pp. 332–66; and, H. H. Jennings, "Sociometric Grouping in Relation to Child Development," in Caroline Tryon (ed.), *Fostering Mental Health in Our Schools* (Washington: Association for Supervision and Curriculum Development, National Education Association, 1950), pp. 203–25.

eighth. He doesn't talk too much. We've never fought or anything, have always got along good.

She helps me—like in social studies, I was afraid to get up and recite. So she checked my paper before class and said the answers were right, and I shouldn't be afraid to say them. That's why I recite more.

Sometimes children are brought together by a common experience or problem in their lives. Such was the case of Jane and Laura in a certain first grade; both came from broken homes and seemed to be attracted to each other because of this fact. Jane, with unselfconscious tact, disclosed the circumstances when she said: "Laura's parents are separated, so my family takes her along when we go places; Laura likes Betty, and I try to please Laura, so the three of us go together." The "family" Jane mentioned did not include both of her own parents, as the teacher already knew.

Whenever a specific set of choices was studied in the light of the conditions prevailing in the classrooms or homerooms in which the tests were given, a rather high degree of psychological sense was noted. Students apparently had a fairly keen awareness of their own emotional needs and recognized the particular demands of the situation in question fairly well. It was clear that while the child society had many independent values in its operating, it was also definitely affected by adult expectation. Most children know and accept the fact that their happiness in class depends in large measure on their ability to make good in what the teacher asks of them. A very common reason for not wanting to sit or work with noisy boys and girls, even if they were good friends outside, was, "He gets me into trouble," or "She talks and fools too much," or "When we are together, I don't get my work done."

There is actually little risk that arrangements based on spontaneous choice will turn out to be unsound either educationally or psychologically. Often there is little risk of their being so, even when the children's wishes seem to run counter to the teacher's judgment. The latter may be unduly influenced· by considerations of academic ability or standard behavior. This is illustrated by one teacher's surprise when she reports:

I found the children saw things in each other which were not connected with their academic rating. Ronald, who had an IQ of 75, was chosen six times. I had always considered Ronald emotionally unstable, immature, and below his grade level. I don't know whether I unconsciously changed toward him, or whether he has just grown these two months, but he reads nicely now, holds his own in class discussion. I wonder whether I can credit the sociogram in making me more aware of the potentialities in Ronald.

Furthermore, when children are allowed to express their own preferences freely, they tend to become more aware of group relations among themselves. They begin to explore each other's minds and personalities and thus start the process of significant interchange. When they have been given such freedom of choice, the evidence—from observation and the children's themes—points to growth in social interaction as well as in personal maturity. Children begin to develop the capacity to see their own and their classmates' qualities in relation to one another. They become more realistic in their expressed wishes and tend to be less given to wishful thinking and to escape into fantasy. They begin to ask for companions who represent an increasing challenge to, or an extension of, their existing selves. But, above all, the phenomenon of group work tends to come into action whereby individuals are helped not only to understand themselves and others, and to give and receive help, but also to develop a sense of joint responsibility for all members of the group and to avoid harsh, punishing attitudes.

This is illustrated by an incident in an elementary class.

One very quiet boy, who had spoken hardly above a whisper all year displayed a great originality in writing a radio part for a play which his new seatmates were preparing. At the first rehearsal, his voice was so utterly toneless that the director threatened to take over. The other boys chorused, "He can do it, let him do it himself!" The spirit and vim which the boy displayed in the final rendition of his lines brought a warranted outburst of applause.

CHARACTERISTIC EMPHASES BY AGE LEVEL

There are certain typical variations in the social patterning according to age levels. Sociograms made in the primary grades, for example, usually consist of several chains of one-way relations with few mutual choices and practically no complex networks. Thus, Mary asks for Jane and Joe, who in turn each ask for other children, who then choose still others. At this stage of their development children are apparently not very conscious of the impression they are making on one another and are relatively self-centered. Shared experience and reciprocated affection do not seem as yet to have the great importance for the individual which they are to have a little later. Difficulties between little children arise largely out of this context of knowing little about each other's feelings. The task of adjusting to other people is one of the big problems in their world.

In kindergarten and first-grade sociograms, furthermore, there are many choice lines between boys and girls (see Figure 5). After the first grade, there is usually a decline in such relations, which continues in the downward direction into the fifth and sixth grades, and then remains fairly constant practically up to the eighth grade. At this level the trend is typically reversed. The number of choices across sex lines increases somewhat every year on through high school and is accompanied by a related increase in the number of reciprocated choices. In fact, mutual affinities appear characteristically at several stages; the number increases sharply in the second, fourth, sixth, and eighth grades, as well as in high school, although during all middle elementary years the association is predominantly between members of the same sex.

Growing interest in, and awareness of, each other results in greater complexity in the sociograms, which reflect this developing social awareness. Thus, beginning in the fifth or the sixth grade, linked chains of mutual association become more frequent and combine to form complicated patterns and clusters. Some of these may be self-contained, and there is a strong tendency for homogeneous cliques to appear (see Figure 6). When children first become thoroughly aware of adult society and their own need to declare their independence of it, they appear to want support from their own kind with especial acuteness. The most immediate accompaniment of this tendency is heightened sex consciousness, but as this yields to increasing need for mutuality, a powerful trend asserts itself for children to prefer companionship with those who share their own ethnic or socioeconomic background, their religion, way of dressing, or ability (or difficulty) in speaking the

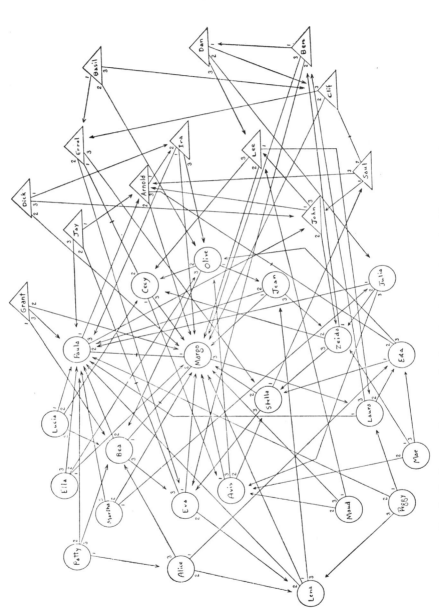

FIG. 5.—Sociogram of a first-grade class, showing usual trends of interpersonal structure.

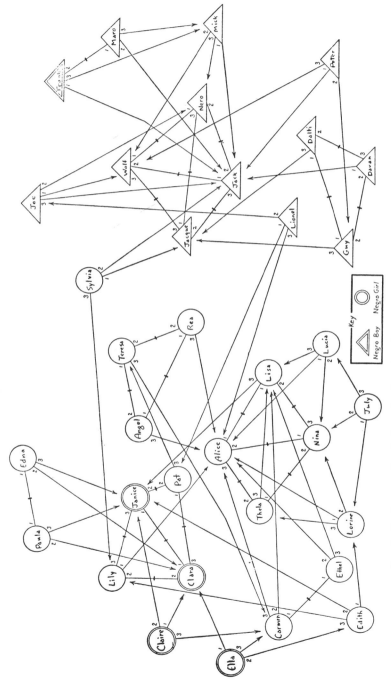

Fig. 6.—Sociogram of a sixth-grade class, showing usual trends of interpersonal structure.

English language. Some patterns may be so closely knit that all choices made and received by their members originate within the circle. Others may be loosely or even quite strongly connected with other sets. The number of highly chosen individuals, and of reciprocated choices between these, tends to increase as the young people grow up. As should perhaps be expected, there appears at each later stage greater variety in the reasons given for wanting to be with classmates and in the range of leadership positions developed within the class. The social structure of each class at every age level thus primarily reflects the students' own regard for one another, and any series of sociograms becomes a record of developing social capacity.

FACTORS IN THE CLASSROOM ATMOSPHERE

Contrary to the usual expectation, the project studies indicate that social structure is by no means affected by age alone. Marked deviations from the generally assumed age-level norms can be brought about by training in human relations. Even the mere permission to interact freely can be enough to bring about changes along certain lines.

In the experience of the project, three factors were identified as promoting social development in the classroom to a significant extent as reflected in sociometric structure. These were the warmth of the teacher, activities which permit a high degree of interaction, and use of democratic methods.

The quality above referred to as the teacher's warmth was found expressed in many ways. Some teachers expressed pleasure and enthusiasm at what happened in the course of the day by remarks such as, "We really made our visitors yesterday feel at home with us." They seemed to take the whole class in at a glance and respond to the moods of individual children: "Is something bothering you, Joe? You look as if you didn't agree with that." Such teachers were usually animated, receptive, and given to quick humor—even at their own expense. Children in their classes were quick to point out any of their intentions that their teacher might have overlooked. When they asked for help, it was to be noted that they had explicit reasons for doing so, and the same observation applied to their interaction with one another. Of further interest was the fact that when children and such teachers met informally in the corridors, they greeted each other spontaneously. Contacts were initiated by children and teachers with equal frequency. The children seemed to extend to one another much the same permissive treatment they got from their teacher. They seemed to expect to hear one another out, and interruptions were checked with such comments as, "Let's wait 'til Bill finishes."

The second factor here under discussion, a program of learning activities based on participation, usually took the form of small group projects. A common theme or topic was agreed upon in general discussion, then the class broke up into intimate small groups for the intensive work, and the results were later reported to the whole class for final conclusions. This procedure seemed to offer girls and boys a chance to know each other's aptitudes and to motivate them to work together toward a common goal. It was the exact opposite in effect from formal classroom methods in that it tended to capitalize upon, rather than disregard, individual differences. Children in different activities were brought together instead of being separated. Important in this connection was the teacher's appreciation of the time element; enough time was always provided for the children to go about their tasks with a sense of ease. Teachers were observed to allow more time for the first stages of any activity than became necessary later on. The time allotment was frequently cut down by the children themselves as their skill in collaboration was sharpened. Likewise, significant was the fact that teachers were always careful to carry out whatever decisions the children had reached, and that the girls and boys observed the same respect for the group decisions of their classmates.

An example is as follows. A class that was going to study the local community began by pooling the questions and ideas that each child had thought important. Somebody wondered "What good will it do us to know these things?" and it was agreed that small groups should take up the proposed list of topics to see which were the most important among them. It then appeared that newcomers to the community wanted to know some things that the others had thought unimportant, that pupils who had moved a good deal expected certain things that old residents hadn't thought of, that children of minority status knew things that surprised some of the others, and that the community did not mean at all the same thing for everybody in the class. This led to the significant question, "How can we find out whether what we think is true is really true?" in the light of which the class project was then planned. The activities finally agreed upon called for different roles for each individual, according to differing skills, temperaments, and interests, all of which were recognized as needed for the job. Competition for tasks was minimized because of the emphasis on many possible contributions. Remarks such as, "You can do it better because you live right there on that street," were frequently heard—sometimes obviously pointing out to a child something he himself had not realized.

The third factor is the use of democratic methods rather consistently. Teachers who proceeded on this principle were observed to put high value on group decisions, to see that differences in opinion were brought out into the open rather than stored up, and to arrange for the expression of all opinions that appeared to be current. They set the stage, as it were, for listening to all sides: they helped each party to identify the facts needed for making points, to clarify impressions, and to formulate conclusions. For example, a child in one of the observed classes, when the local community was being discussed, remarked, "I've heard that the Jews have all the money!" The members of the class quickly showed signs of pouncing on the boy, but before they could do so, the teacher pointed out, "If Arthur hadn't told us what he had heard, we wouldn't be able to look into whether it is so or not!" The emphasis shifted at once from antagonism to an eager questioning: "Who told you?" "Who said that?" Protection of minority opinion by focusing on the issue rather than on the person expressing it was a consistent characteristic of such teachers' classroom practices.

The above illustrations show that the devices used for setting a positive atmosphere are rather simple and require no major reorganization of ways of working. Comments such as, "Are all suggestions in?" "What would you like to come of this?" consistently used, seemed to prevent arbitrary and dominating behavior. Consistent focusing on issues rather than on personal opinions prepared for a way both to utilize differences and to view them objectively.

Observation in the cooperating schools did not indicate that all three of the major factors discussed above were always equally present when the social structure surpassed the development usual at the given level. Strength in one of the three sometimes, however, appeared to make up for almost total absence of the others; warmth in approach was observed in a few cases to compensate appreciably for lack of group activities; democratic fairness was likewise seen to make up in large measure, at times, for relative coldness or formality. In most cases, however, teachers who were seen to create a warm atmosphere were also the ones who liked activity programs and employed democratic procedures. There was, therefore, little opportunity to study the impact of each of the three factors singly in the absence of the other two.

SOME CHARACTERISTICS OF ASSOCIATION PATTERNS

What the pattern of association may look like under conditions that allow for living space along the lines described above is shown in Figures 7 and 8.

The first, Figure 7, shows the structure among six-year-old children in a first grade. It will be seen that there is a high number of reciprocated choices, some of them linking many children into a network, that several children received a great number of choices, and that many girls and boys in the least-prominent positions asked to be with those of their classmates who were most chosen. There are many boy-girl choices. This broad and inclusive pattern differs significantly in all the above respects from the results obtained in most first-grade classrooms. In fact, it is unlike the typical sociogram for this grade as described in the preceding section (see Figure 5, p. 76), except in the large number of choices it records between girls and boys. The relative maturity or degree of social integration shown is similar to that found in many eighth grades under so-called "normal" conditions, and, indeed, surpasses some of those on record.

The second sociogram, Figure 8, shows the structure of a sixth grade. There is a broad spread of much-chosen positions, many links among them, and some between the prominently located

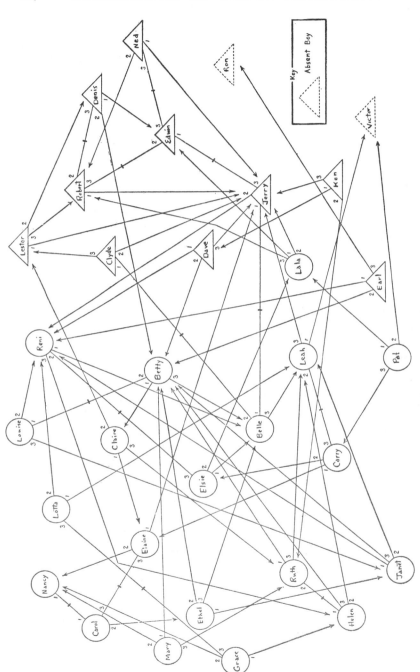

Fig. 7.—Sociogram of a first-grade class, showing interpersonal structure under an atmosphere promoting interaction. Only occasionally will a child use fewer than the full number of choices (see Nancy).

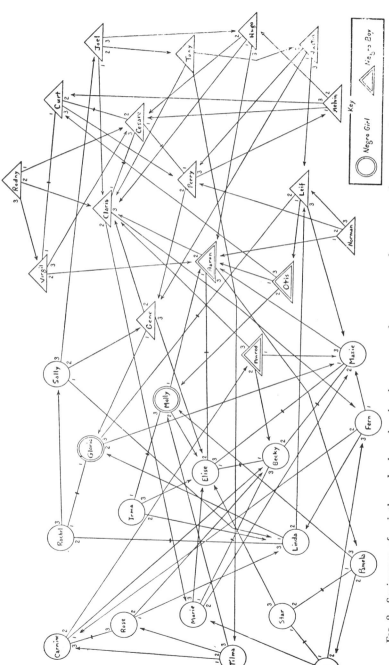

Fig. 8.—Sociogram of a sixth-grade class, showing interpersonal structure under an atmosphere promoting interaction.

boys and girls. Negro children are as well integrated as the rest. The intersex cleavage and the tendency toward closed formations usual at this age do not appear.

Patterns of social relations like either of the above mean that communication lines are open throughout the group, among all members, directly and indirectly, so that ideas and feelings can be widely shared. They also reflect a certain readiness to recognize individual differences, since much-chosen positions are accorded to a variety of children. Furthermore, the structure throughout makes it possible for the least prominent members of the group to find spokesmen or to speak up for themselves and get a hearing. The patterns also point to the absence of static roles; when relations are so varied and so broad, there is little occasion to follow the line of least resistance and simply pair off or associate exclusively with the same individuals.

The above examples illustrate how strongly the classroom atmosphere can modify what are usually considered to be typical structures of interrelationships of school children at various developmental levels. There is another side of the picture that bears on the same point from the opposite direction. When the classroom atmosphere is repressive, the sociometric evidence shows up retardation in social structure below the expected norm and, also, distortion of the usual patterns.

Figure 9 depicts the structure in a fifth grade. In this classroom a premium was placed on obedience and keeping quiet. Permission had to be asked even for such minor things as sharpening a pencil. On the score of interacting, the girls and boys did little more than exchange glances, and the teacher rarely responded to a class on other than a strictly business basis. Her, "Will row one get ready to leave!" at the end of school was more like a general announcement than a statement to the children; their response took the form simply of leaving promptly. Misdemeanors were punished by making the youngsters pray after school or write a hundred times such sentences as "I have been careless." The physical arrangements minimized, if they did not actually destroy, social give and take. The teacher allowed her pupils to sit where they wanted to for the first two weeks of the term, and then reassigned them herself on the basis of good and bad behavior, the criterion

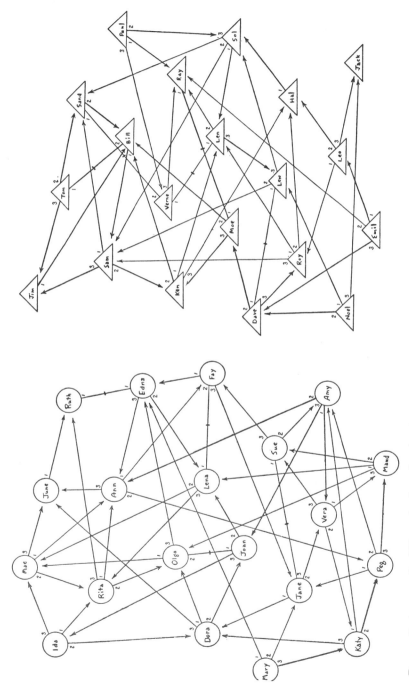

Fig. 9.—Sociogram of a fifth-grade class, showing interpersonal structure under an atmosphere restricting interaction. Note that many of the children in this class have not used their full choice allowance, and one, Jack, has chosen no one.

being the amount of talking that had taken place. In the end each child was placed as far away as possible from those to whom he felt most attracted. Work was always assigned by the teacher and carried out by each child alone. Praise was given for ability to accomplish tasks individually, for not disturbing the others, and for being "self-sufficient." In the halls the teacher was seen to speak to no child and no child to speak to her. As far as could be observed, there were no legitimate occasions in school for informal communication between them at all.

This last sociogram is not like ones usually found in any grade; it depicts, in addition, a very marked distortion of the typical structure for this level of development. Among the forty children, it will be noted, one-way choices predominate, and there are actually fewer reciprocated choices than are usually found in the first grade. The lines of choice do not come together in an integrated pattern or focus on particular individuals in any way. There appears to be a continuous reaching out that cannot even produce the cliques so often evolved by children of this age. The atmosphere may have been so hostile to social contacts that no personalities could make themselves known. Even the usual forms of communication for which children risk penalties appeared to have been inhibited. The picture seems to suggest that when children do not value what the teacher emphasizes and at the same time cannot for one reason or another express their predicament, they tend to "sit out" the regime to which they are subjected.

As these examples show, the patterns of cross-sex choice, closed groups, reciprocated choice, and the like, that are usually found at different ages under prevailing conditions, do not persist when the atmosphere is encouraging to interaction. This means that the usual patterns need not become dominant. The structure of children's interaction tends to be as broad and inclusive as the environment permits and the educational milieu invites.

SUMMARY

A setting in which social interaction can flourish and mature makes possible many kinds of learning that are crucial to the development of citizens in a modern democracy. Boys and girls can become skilled in the process of group decision, in the exercise of collaboration, and in their acceptance of different personalities and cultural outlooks. They gain perspective on themselves and come to enjoy other individualities for the stimulating variety they offer. Children can learn to appraise their own capacities and learn to make their special aptitudes fit into a larger scheme in combination with the talents of others. They can experience the satisfaction and peculiar thrill of teamwork and group enterprise. In short, they can learn what it means to do things together.

It is important to stress, in this connection, that there is something personally and emotionally expanding about this type of learning. As children participate as active agents, they become aware of what group procedure can mean. The great significance of sociometric methods, at this point, lies in the opportunity they afford teachers to create a predisposition for active give and take. Teachers usually find such classrooms easy to work with and generally responsive. Work projects can be initiated at any point in the known network of pupils' affinities and readily extended to include other members of the class. Under such conditions children develop considerable appreciation of and interest in different viewpoints with surprising ease; their sympathies come into action with very little prompting. When their most immediate psychological needs are adequately met, they can—and usually do—start reaching out toward more varied and challenging contacts. While children act in the direction of preserving themselves as persons, the opportunities provided for them in the school can free them to become workers, learners, or effective group members unhampered by the private, personalized concerns. In short, a child's capacity for social growth—his ability to live with his fellows to the full—is as natural and as educable as his other basic capacities for mental and physical growth. As such, the capacity for social growth must be considered an essential concern for the school curriculum.

V. PSYCHOLOGICAL THEORY OF SOCIOMETRIC CHOICES

CHILDREN'S USE OF CHOICE IS REVEALED UPON INVESTIGATION through projective techniques and interviews to be characterized by the chooser seeking appropriate interpersonal experience with another who is able and willing to help with developmental problems he considers himself to be facing. In making his choice he may be quite unaware that he is using this criterion and also largely unaware of the significance of his choice behavior. His first choice—the one that he makes with the highest degree of discrimination—is found to be aimed particularly at finding help to grow toward maturity in handling his problems. This does not mean that the person chosen is more mature in all respects than the chooser, but that the chosen is capable and willing to be of spontaneous assistance in the current maturation problem of the chooser.

THE PSYCHOLOGICAL STAIRCASE PHENOMENON

A child's choices are found to be graduated: he selects others who are, at their stages of development, more skillful in meeting the special situations and problems confronting him, or who have greater confidence and better contact with specific elements in situations which are troubling him, or who, by temperament, are able· to help him see life more optimistically and zestfully. It is this phenomenon that the writer has named the "psychological staircase phenomenon of sociometric structure."

Thus, the chosen will not be at a great psychological distance from the chooser; he will be sufficiently more advanced in respect to matters of importance to the chooser that he can help without being impatient or unconcerned; the chosen will be close enough to the chooser in development so that his attitude is marked, not by condescension or boredom, but by constant, dependable, and keen interest. In brief, emotional comprehension must be present.

A few examples from children's interviews regarding their first choices, which follow, are brief but typical illustrations:

Well, I act silly because I'm nervous, and he acts silly out of being glad. He's always showing me how to hold on to myself.

He's above most people in conquering things that have happened to him, the same things have happened to me. Gee! Can he take it!

When I come to school and I don't feel too good, she will cheer me up and she is always a pal; she is always happy and she makes others happy too. When I'm with her she cheers me up.

The psychological staircase phenomenon can account for the fact that first choices have a greater stability and a longer duration than second or lower degrees of choice. The chooser makes his greatest psychological investment in his first choice, reaching deep into the core of his personality in making his decision, and apparently this choice can be neither outgrown nor replaced as readily or as quickly as his other choices, which are less essential and less necessary to him. While for some individuals every choice has a depth value and while all choices (of any degree) are of importance to the chooser and the chosen, the implications of crucial needs lie chiefly in first choices.

In the cases studied it has been noted that only a small percentage of the children do not reveal a gain in growth by their successive selections. In this phenomenon two trends are apparent. One can be called "horizontal choosing," since it appears to reflect desire to remain on a plateau; the selections appear to be aimed at assuring an approval of the *status quo* without the irritation of stimulation toward increasing maturity. Such choosing is a serious deviation and, if it recurs persistently, suggests that the child is under pressure to consolidate and hold onto the level of maturity he has reached. Unless he is given enough aid to pull himself away from plateau choosing, his social-emotional progress may even be retarded and he may slip into a still less desirable pattern of choosing—that of regressive choosing or making what can be called "cellar" choices. That is, he may tend to select associates who will allow him to slip back to an earlier stage of his growth, or, worse, distort or destroy the direction of his development.

Both tendencies—to horizontal choosing and to regressive choosing—are indications of considerable emotional disturbance, and care must be taken to help the child overcome either choice behavior, and here it may be necessary to call upon the services of a child guidance clinic or other community agency. The teacher, however, must realize that the child's choice is based on his needs and that separating him physically from his choices will not provide a "cure" for him. In fact, separation may serve only to enhance the chosen in the eyes of the child. The teacher can be constructive by arranging placement so that it provides the child with some of his choices *at the same time* that it places him with others who can "open his eyes." For example, if a child who is very indecisive, highly suggestible, readily dominated, and self-deprecating chooses associates who make of others an outlet for their own needs to persecute, then he should still be given placement with one of his choices, but the two should be placed with several other children who are wholesomely able to expand the horizons of both dominated and dominator. In such a setting the latter are exposed to day-by-day experiences which can offer them opportunity to develop insight into the fruitless returns of their behavior and encouragement toward constructive growth.

However psychologically astute the teacher may be in working out the most helpful sociometric placement for the few pupils who are given to plateau or regressive choosing, it must be remembered that even ideal placement cannot be expected to undo quickly what may have been years in the building; still it can provide for motivational change and act as a deterrent to further deterioration of adjustment.

THE PSYCHOLOGICAL STAIRCASE AND DISCRIMINATION IN MAKING CHOICES

Discrimination in choosing according to the problem posed by the sociometric question (criterion) occurs within the context of the demands of the phenomenon of the psychological staircase. Children appear to use their choices above all else to preserve and build themselves as *persons*. When the school setting provides sufficient opportunity for them to gain this satisfaction, then they show themselves as being able to differentiate spontaneously in their choices according to whether the situation is "collective" (that is, calls for common endeavor in a stated activity or activities) or "noncollective" (that is, permits individual pupils to determine how they will use their time and efforts). When children are given ample opportunity to interact, they will gradually show greater and greater ability to choose appropriately for the situation proposed by the sociometric question, always, however, within the general pattern of their age group and developmental level.

Thus, the younger the children, the greater the overlap between their choices regardless of criterion. But even in the primary grades, given a constructive setting, children will come more and more to differentiate between their sociometric choices for recreational periods or seating arrangements and making their choices for specific projects, with a developing sense of task orientation. They show themselves to become increasingly able to appraise critically the abilities needed to carry out the task posed, and in particular ways they seek to complement one another. Thus, as one child phrased it, "He knows how to plan it out so we don't get stuck, and he figures and you figure till it comes together, more complete."

PSYCHEGROUP AND SOCIOGROUP CONTINUUM

If sociometric opportunity is given only in "common goals" situations (as in studying chemistry or mathematics in a class) and opportunities for person-to-person contacts are limited, it can be expected that pupils will try to see and be with the individuals who mean most to them in a personal sense. Under these circumstances it is impossible to determine the extent to which the interpersonal structure might have been different had the pupils had other, planned opportunities during the school day to associate informally according to their own desires.

The collective and noncollective patterns of association are essentially different in structure, function, and significance, although there is almost always some degree of overlap between them. The one pattern, called a *psychegroup,* is based on the needs of individuals to interact with one another and permits each individual as a unique personality to be appreciated and given consideration by those whom he chooses, with varying degrees of spontaneous indulgence and affection. This association pattern may be said to be based upon the counting "altogether" as a person in the esteem and regard of the other participants. The other association pattern, called a *sociogroup,* is oriented to the collective group setting and the accomplishments of its collective aims.

The focus in sociometric structure that develops in the *sociogroup* is upon the individual's role in the activities which are considered the group's official responsibility (for example, in an algebra class, the responsibility: to learn algebra). In the psychegroup the focus is upon the members' person-to-person responsiveness to one another; there is no official obligation for the members to associate with one another or to achieve any common objective agreed upon in advance.

Research on individuals at the adult and near-adult levels discloses a very clear picture of differentiation in choice expression, resulting in the psychegroup and the sociogroup as two ends of a continuum. Along this continuum certain kinds of grouping show degrees of similarity to the sociometric patterns found at the two extremes, depending on whether the criterion (sociometric question) reflects more or less emphasis upon the personalized role or the impersonalized role[1] in the interaction called for.

Only when one group of children is studied for *each* of these patterns does their importance to the mental hygiene of personal development become clear. The pattern of psychegroup relations is best displayed in a sociogram whose criterion allows the child to select others simply for close association in an informal setting, for example, when the criterion is *sitting nearby in homeroom.* The structure of sociogroup relations can be determined through the use of criteria appropriate to collective situations of a more formal sort, as *working on the same committee in social studies.* The differences in alignment of the interrelations among the mem-

---

[1] Helen Hall Jennings, "Structural Differences in Groups: The Psychegroup and the Sociogroup," *Leadership and Isolation* (2nd ed.; New York: Longmans, Green, 1950), pp. 274–302.

bers show clearly when comparison is made of their official groups, so formed, with their unofficial groups, where person-to-person responsiveness alone is paramount.

Figures 10 and 11 show two sociograms of an eighth-grade class, based on two criteria—homeroom seating and working on mathematics. A comparison of the two sociograms reveals some of the differences which may be expected to appear in choice structure when one criterion calls for personality-to-personality interaction (psychegroup motivation) and the other criterion calls for interaction in which specialized skills are important. It should be added that the group here being considered had been accustomed to considerable autonomy in forming their association patterns and in communicating with one another. Thus, it will be noted that nearly all members differentiated between those they chose on each criterion, or at least differentiated in the degree of choice for particular individuals, in the contrasting situations. At the same time the mathematics sociogram is shown to be more "pinnacled" —a few individuals are much chosen, and a greater number are unchosen than in the homeroom-seating sociogram.[2] In the mathematics sociogram the pupils' ranking of one another in their choices of co-workers in mathematics parallels closely the teacher's ranking of pupils for ability, interest, and performance in mathematics.

In a sociogroup setting (in this case, mathematics) the overwhelming choice expression focused upon a relatively small proportion of the group members. Here the many individuals left unchosen do not, of course, indicate poor adjustment; the pattern is simply an indication that throughout the group as a whole there is appreciation and recognition of those members who are best able and most willing to aid other members in the particular tasks that are the official obligation of the group.

It is clear that every sociogram has to be interpreted within the setting of the community in which its population lives and functions. Moreover, no one aspect of a sociogram (for example, the number of unchosen) can be taken as a sole index of any given group's manner of functioning.

[2] *Ibid.*, p. 266. In the community generally the individual finds greater difficulty in winning psychegroup choice than he does sociogroup choice.

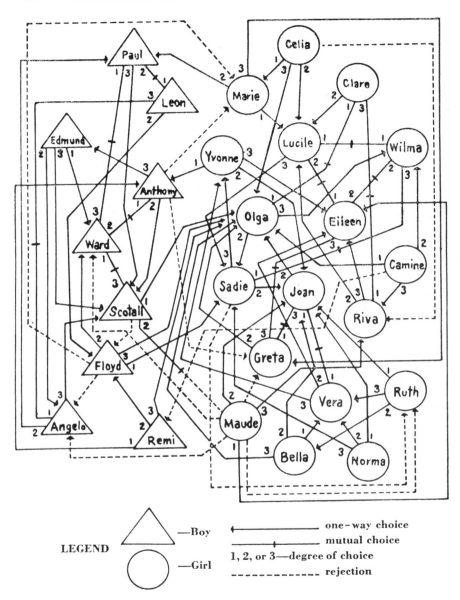

FIG. 10.—Sociogram of an eighth-grade class, showing psychegroup inter-action. The sociometric criterion was homeroom seating.

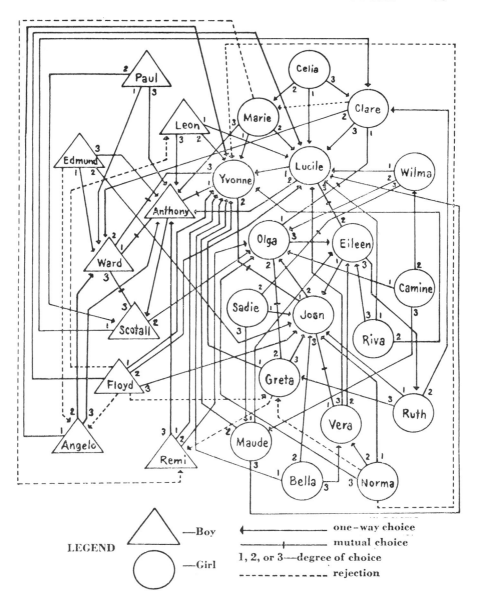

LEGEND

△ —Boy

◯ —Girl

⟵———— one-way choice

—————┼———— mutual choice

1, 2, or 3—degree of choice

- - - - - - - - - rejection

Fig. 11.—Sociogram of an eighth-grade class, showing sociogroup motivation. The sociometric criterion was working on mathematics.

THE NECESSITY FOR PSYCHEGROUP SATISFACTION

Exchange on a *personal* basis appears to be a fundamental need of the child; if this need is not fulfilled, the individual is hampered in developing other kinds of association, such as collaboration in work and study. Discrimination in making choices for sociogroup work is apparently easier for the child when at the same time he has interaction with and acceptance by others in group settings that call for no academic or special skills.[3] It is as if, through satisfactions coming to the child as a *person,* he is freed to think of the official objectives of the group and is better able to function as a learner and a worker, relatively detached from more personalized concerns. He seems to have less need to bring private interpersonal relations into situations in which they are not a consideration of the group endeavor. Thus, if children are to develop the capacity to relate themselves to others satisfactorily in a sociogroup setting (in learning to read adequately, spell, and so on), it is necessary that at the same time they have opportunity as individuals to sustain themselves individually on a person-to-person basis through interaction satisfying to them as persons.

Thus, the extent of the overlap of choices made in response to contrasting criteria is an index of the functioning of the group-life program of the school in meeting the psychegroup needs of the children. The less extensive the overlap, the more suitable the program may be inferred to be in enabling the children to grow up emotionally and socially and to participate with others in many kinds of group situations.

Apparently the child only gradually achieves the ability to relate to others selectively in terms of the kind of situation confronting him. Age and past experiences in interpersonal relations, as well as the immediate atmosphere of the group situation, affect the child's progress in using his choice potential. To expect the child to be a worker when he does not also have the chance to be a person (by his definition) is tantamount to ordering a reversal of the psychological sequence which sociometric findings reveal as characteristic of child development.

Sociometric study indicates that the child's first responsibility

---

[3] Similar findings appear at the adult level; see *ibid.,* and, particularly, Paul Maucorps, "A Sociometric Inquiry in the French Army," *Sociometry,* XII (February 1949), 46–80.

is to his evolving self, his needs, and his longings for interplay with others, who, because they are also involved in the same absorbing process of ego construction, comprehend, accept, and encourage him. Apparently, in the midst of this great developmental task, unless the child concurrently has relationships that help him in this task with some degree of satisfaction, he turns only with great reluctance to the secondary job of applying himself to sociogroup tasks and skills.

The need to be respected as a person thus seems to be important for the child's psychology of choice. Any method of grouping which is interpreted by the child as generally disparaging to his prestige and self-esteem affects his spontaneity in using his sociometric choices. For example, in schools in which graduated ability grouping[4] is practiced, the children, too, practice hierarchical sociometric sectioning. At the lowest level of the pyramid even intragroup relations appear to be sparse, as if the children in this category look upon each other as undesirables.

Sociometric findings suggest that when children are very young, they are largely unaware of where they stand with other children. But awareness sharpens as they grow older, as each succeeding year brings with it keener insight.

In locations, for example, where children become affected by racial prejudice, as they grow older they withdraw into their own racial group for intimate relationships.[5] The result is a narrowing of the field of choice within which the psychological staircase phenomenon operates. In looking for those who can aid their growth toward maturity, the members of each group make choices, not from the class as a whole, but from their own racial group. A simi-

[4] Even under present testing systems, such grouping is only approximate and fraught with errors. This, however, is largely unknown to the children, and, indeed, to the teachers in many instances; in sectioning it is taken as a settled matter that in a generalized way such and such children are more able than other children.

". . . testing procedures unwisely used can do harm. A few basic considerations must be understood: First, tests are effective on a limited front. Second, no single test should become a basis for important decisions. Third, test scores are one kind of data to be placed alongside other kinds of data." [and] "The most effective educational system can be defeated by a social environment that blunts or destroys aspiration." From *The Pursuit of Excellence: Education and the Future of America,* prepared by Panel V of the Special Studies Project of the Rockefeller Brothers Fund, Inc. (Reported in *New York Times,* June 23, 1958, p. 16).

[5] Joan H. Criswell, "A Sociometric Study of Race Cleavage in the Classroom," *Archives of Psychology,* No. 235, January 1939.

lar limitation of the field of choice is found where socioclass differences among children distort the extent and kind of relationships they feel free to develop. Hence, in this case, too, the quality
of individual development is adversely affected.[6]

ASSESSMENT OF CHOICE AND GROUP STRUCTURE

Before sociometric tests came into use, it was not so clear what
effect various grouping arrangements within the classroom and
between classrooms were having upon social relationships of children and, in turn, upon their self-confidence, upon view of themselves, and upon their roles as learners. It is now apparent that a
method of grouping which systematically utilizes the children's
own efforts to socialize through interaction with one another can
be a great vehicle toward development.

Individuals have different potentials for interpersonal affiliation
and each has his own individuality of expression, both for attract-
ing others and for accepting response from them. It is important
that this individuality be respected—not compared or judged by
someone else's pattern or any "average" pattern. Individuality in
choice expression represents the child's feelings *as of now*—feelings
which may be fulfilling or feelings which he may need help in
outgrowing. So, too, the potential and the individuality of any
group structure needs to be understood in relation to its setting,
its criterion, its age level, and the goals of its members in order to
comprehend their bearing on the patterning of the group,

Group work and use of the sociometric technique should go
hand in hand; both are educative measures that enable individuals, when grouped together, to grow toward a maturer individual
and group life. While "group" and "individual" in this sense can
be separated from each other only theoretically, group life cannot
be better than the quality of the interpersonal relationships individuals develop.[7] Unless the structures that individuals build in

[6] Paul H. Maucorps, "Sympathy and Empathy: A Perceptual Study of Children's
and Adolescents' Social Relations" (Centre National de la Recherche Scientifique,
Paris). See also Arthur T. Jersild, *Child Psychology* (4th ed.; New York: Prentice-
Hall, Inc. 1954), especially chap. viii.

[7] Grace L. Coyle, *Group Work with American Youth* (New York: Harper & Bros.
1948); and Herbert A. Thelen, *Dynamics of Groups at Work* (Chicago: University
of Chicago Press, 1954).

response to one another are appreciated, recognized, and allowed to grow broader and deeper, the individuals themselves cannot feel motivated to gain the social development that is possible for them. These structures are the social soil in which any educational or institutional program is most effectively planted.

The teacher may be said to have the especial role of sociometric mentor: that of encouraging students' genuinely felt and genuinely needed choices to find expression, so that by augmenting their experience, their choice potential may take on a creative role in their own life situations. For the teacher this becomes a matter of aiding the individual to gain or regain confidence in his use of choice and in his reception of choice, to *dare* to exercise choice when this aspect of his growth has been neglected, blocked, or undermined in other settings, sometimes prior to school experience or, even, within prior school experience.

BIBLIOGRAPHY

The following publications of the American Council on Education describe sociometric methods used in various programs of curricula and school life in many places.

Curriculum in Intergroup Relations: Case Studies in Instruction for Secondary Schools. By Hilda Taba, Elizabeth Hall Brady, Helen Hall Jennings, John T. Robinson, and Flora Dolton. 1949.

Diagnosing Human Relations Needs. By Hilda Taba, Elizabeth Hall Brady, John T. Robinson, and William E. Vickery. 1951.

Elementary Curriculum in Intergroup Relations. By Hilda Taba, Elizabeth Hall Brady, John T. Robinson, and Flora Dolton. 1950.

Intergroup Education in Public Schools. By Hilda Taba, Elizabeth Hall Brady, and John T. Robinson. 1952.

Literature for Human Understanding. By Hilda Taba. 1948.

School Culture: Studies of Participation and Leadership. By Hilda Taba. 1955.

With Focus on Human Relations. By Hilda Taba and Deborah Elkins. 1950.

With Perspective on Human Relations: A Study of Peer Group Dynamics in an Eighth Grade. By Hilda Taba. 1955.

GENERAL BIBLIOGRAPHY

ADLER, ALFRED. *The Education of the Individual.* New York: Philosophical Library, 1958.

BJERSTEDT, AKE. "The Methodology of Preferential Sociometry," *Sociometry Monographs,* No. 37. New York: Beacon House, 1956.

BONNEY, MERL E. "Personality Traits of Socially Successful and Socially Unsuccessful Children," *Journal of Educational Psychology,* XXXIV (1943), 449–72.

———. "Social Behavior Differences between Second Grade Children of High and Low Sociometric Status," *Journal of Educational Research,* XLVIII (1955), 481–95.

BORGATTA, E. F. "Analysis of Social Interaction and Sociometric Perception," *Sociometry,* XVII (1954), 7–32.

BROWNE, C. G., and COHN, THOMAS S. (eds.). *The Study of Leadership.* Danville, Ill.: Interstate Printers & Publishers, 1958.

Bulletin of the Institute of Child Study. Toronto, Canada: University of Toronto Press. [Useful to any teacher through its suggestions of ways to help children grow socially.]

CALABRIA, FRANK M. "Psyche and Socio Group Process and Structure in Recreation Settings," to be published in *International Journal of Sociometry and Sociatry*, Vol. IV.

CLAMPITT, RICHARD R., and CHARLES, DON C. "Sociometric Status and Supervisory Evaluation of Institutionalized Mentally Deficient Children," *Journal of Social Psychology*, XLIV (1956), 223–31.

COYLE, GRACE L. *Group Work with American Youth*. New York: Harper & Bros., 1948.

CRISWELL, JOAN H. "The Measurement of Group Integration," *Sociometry*, X (1947), 259–69.

———. "Sociometric Study of Race Cleavage in the Classroom," *Archives of Psychology*, No. 235 (January 1939).

ELKINS, DEBORAH. "Some Factors Related to the Choice-Status of Ninety Eighth-Grade Children in a School Society," *Genetic Psychology Monographs*, LVIII, 207–72. Provincetown, Mass.: Journal Press, 1958.

FEINBERG, MORTIMER R.; SMITH, MAX; and SCHMIDT, ROBERT. "An Analysis of Expressions Used by Adolescents at Varying Economic Levels To Describe Accepted and Rejected Peers," *Journal of Genetic Psychology*, XCIII (1958), 133–48.

HEATON, MARGARET M., and LEWIS, HELEN B. *Reading Ladders for Human Relations*. 2nd ed., revised and enlarged. Washington: American Council on Education, 1955.

HOHN, E., and SCHICK, C. P. *Das Soziogramm*. Stuttgart: Testverlag Siegfried Wolf, 1954.

HUREWITZ, PAUL. "Sociometric Investigation of the Isolate," to be published in *International Journal of Sociometry and Sociatry*, Vol. III.

HUSQUINET, ALBERT. *L'adaptation scolaire et familiale des jeunes garçons de 12 à 14 ans d'après le test sociométrique et le test d'aperception thématique*. Paris: Société d'Edition "Les Belles Lettres," 1954.

JENNINGS, HELEN HALL. "The Choosing Process," *Reader of Sociometry*. Glencoe, Ill.: Glencoe Free Press, 1959.

———. *Leadership and Isolation*. 2nd ed. New York: Longmans, Green, 1950.

———. "Sociometric Structure in Personality and Group Formation," in Muzafer Sherif and M. O. Wilson (eds.), *Group Relations at the Crossroads*, pp. 332–66. New York: Harper & Bros., 1953.

———. "Sociometric Grouping in Relation to Child Development" and "Sociodrama as Educative Process" [bearing on human development], pp. 203–25, 260–85, in Caroline Tryon (ed.), *Fostering Mental Health in Our Schools*. Washington: Association for Supervision and Curriculum Development, National Education Association, 1950.

———. "Sociometry," in Philip Lawrence Harriman (ed.), *Encyclopedia of Psychology*, p. 874. New York: Philosophical Library, 1946.

JENNINGS, HELEN HALL, in association with TABA, HILDA. *Schule und Schülergemeinschaft*. Deutsch herausgeg. und eingel. von E. Lichtenstein. Berlin-Hamburg: Christian-Verlag, 1951.

JERSILD, ARTHUR T. *Child Psychology*. 4th ed. New York: Prentice-Hall, 1954.

KENWORTHY, LEONARD S. *Introducing Children to the World*. New York: Harper & Bros., 1956.

LINDZEY, GARDNER, and BORGATTA, EDGAR F. "Sociometric Measurement," in G. Lindzey (ed.), *Handbook of Social Psychology*, Vol. I, chap. xi, pp. 405–48. Cambridge, Mass.: Addison-Wellesley Publishing Co., 1954.

LINDZEY, GARDNER, and URDAN, J. A. "Personality and Social Choice," *Sociometry*, XVII (1954), 47–63.

MAUCORPS, PAUL H. "A Sociometric Inquiry in the French Army," *Sociometry*, XII (1949), 46–80.

———. "Sympathy and Empathy: A Perceptual Study of Children's and Adolescents' Social Relations." Paris: Centre National de la Recherche Scientifique, 1958.

MORENO, J. L. *Who Shall Survive? A New Approach to the Problem of Human Interrelations.* Collaborator: H. H. JENNINGS. 1st ed. Washington: Nervous and Mental Disease Publishing Co., 1934. 2nd ed. New York: Beacon House, 1953.

MORENO, J. L., and JENNINGS, HELEN HALL. "Sociometric Control Studies of Grouping and Regrouping," *Sociometry Monographs*, No. 7. New York: Beacon House, 1947.

NEUGARTEN, BERNICE L. "Social Class and Friendship among School Children," *American Journal of Sociology*, LI (1946), 305–13.

NORTHWAY, MARY L. "A Plan for Sociometric Studies in a Longitudinal Programme of Research in Child Development," *Sociometry*, XVII (1954), 272–81.

———. *A Primer of Sociometry.* Toronto, Canada: University of Toronto Press, 1952.

NORTHWAY, MARY L. Chairman, Editorial Committee (Institute of Child Study). *Twenty-five Years of Child Study.* Toronto: University of Toronto Press, 1951.

NORTHWAY, MARY L., and WELD, LINDSAY. *Sociometric Testing: A Guide for Teachers.* Toronto, Canada: University of Toronto Press, 1957.

TABA, HILDA, et al. See publications of American Council on Education listed above.

TAGIURI, R. "Relational Analysis: An Extension of Sociometric Method with Emphasis upon Social Perception," *Sociometry*, XV (1952), 91–104.

TEIRICH, H. R. "Sociometry in Groups," *International Journal of Social Psychiatry*, IV (Summer 1958), 55–61.

THELEN, HERBERT A. *Dynamics of Groups at Work.* Chicago: University of Chicago Press, 1954.

WASHBURNE, CARLETON. *The World's Good: Education for World-Mindedness.* New York: John Day, 1954.

WATTENBERG, WILLIAM W. *The Adolescent Years.* New York: Harcourt, Brace, & Co. 1955.

ZELENY, L. D. "Selection of Compatible Flying Partners," *American Journal of Sociology*, LII (1947), 424–31.

INDEX

Adult sociometric choice, 92, 96n
Assisting individual children, 52–55, 59–60
Association for Supervision and Curriculum Development of National Education Association, viii

Bjerstedt, Ake, viii

"Cellar" choices, 89–90
Chains, sociometric, 27–29
Choice distributions, 22
Choice patterns, factors affecting
  activities permitting interaction, 78–79
  codes, 29, 32, 37
  democratic teaching methods, 78, 80
  home position, 43–44
  physical arrangements, 14, 32, 33, 55–56
  racial prejudice, 97
  repressive classroom atmosphere, 81–86
  sectioning, 97
  self-defense, 28, 40, 86
  skills, value put on, 28
  socioeconomic, 32
  socioclass, 98
  temperament, 28, 59, 88
  traditions, 28, 33, 37–38
  unequal opportunity, 32
  warmth of teacher, 78–79
  See also Psychegroup; Sociogroup
Cleavage
  some sources of, 32–34, 37–38
  study of, 61, 70
  treating, 66–70
Cliques or closed groups, 28, 30, 32, 86
Confidentiality of sociometric results, 19, 20
  maintaining, in operation, 49–50, 67, 70
  violation of, 19

Coyle, Grace L., 98n
Criswell, J., 22n, 97n

Diaries, 40
Differentiation in choice, 91–93, 96
  first choices, 88–89
Discrimination. See Differentiation in choice

Elkins, Deborah, 12n
Emotional disturbance and choice, 89–90

Friendship, not sociometric criterion, 11, 17

Grade-wide sociometric analysis. See Sociometric analysis
Group life and personal development, 1–2, 4–5, 7–10, 78–81, 84–87, 97–99
Group relations and education, 1–10, 87, 98–99
Group work and sociometric technique, 17, 98
Grouping practices
  artificial, 5–6, 90
  graduated ability, 9, 97
  homogeneous, 8–10

Heaton, Margaret M., 54n
Homogeneous grouping. See Grouping practices
"Horizontal choosing," 89–90
Husquinet, Albert, viii

Integrating sociometric structure, 29–31
Intergroup Education project, v, 62, 71

Interviews, home. *See* Teacher's Home
　　Interview Schedule
Interviews on motivations for choice, 34
　　directions for oral, 35–36
　　directions for written, 38–39

Jennings, Helen Hall, 11, 38n, 72n, 92,
　　93
Jersild, Arthur, 98n

Learning
　　academic, inseparable from social, 4,
　　　97
　　effects of overemphasis on individual
　　　on, 4
　　roles in group life and, 4, 6, 7, 86–87
Lewis, Helen B., 54n

Maucorps, Paul, viii, 96n, 98
Moreno, J. D., 22, 102

National Conference of Christians and
　　Jews, v
　　Commission on Educational Organiza-
　　　tions of, v
Negro-white sociometric choice, 22
Networks, extending, 28–30
Northway, Mary L., viii, 36

Observation, 12–13, 47
Open questions and themes, exploring
　　choice meaning, 39
Overlap in choices, 91–92
　　meaning of, 96

Plateau choosing. *See* "Horizontal choos-
　　ing"
Pope, Loren B., 9n
Prejudice
　　creating of, by grouping practices, 8–
　　　10
　　in fostering exclusiveness, 4
　　racial, effects on choice, 97
　　segregation by intelligence tests and,
　　　9, 97
Principles of sociometric placement, 48–
　　51, 58–59, 67, 70, 90
Psychegroup, 91–98
　　and sociogroup continuum, 91–93

Psychegroup—*Continued*
　　choices, difficulty of, compared with
　　　sociogroup, 93n
　　necessity for satisfactions of, 96–98
　　personal orientation of, 92, 96
Psychological sequence of choice, 96–97
Psychological staircase phenomenon of
　　choice, 88–90

Refraining from choosing. *See* Validity
　　of choices
Regressive choosing, 89–90
Rejections (negative choice)
　　caused by academic segregation, 33
　　caused by prejudice, 34
　　directions for securing, 17–18, 20
　　emphases on two-way nature of, 17
　　insight into, 36–39, 47, 52, 54
Reshaping general practices, 55–58
"Rockefeller Report" (Special Studies
　　Project of Rockefeller Brothers
　　Fund, Inc.), 9n, 97n

Sample sociogram form. *See* Sociogram
School-wide sociometric analysis. *See*
　　Sociometric analysis
Sherif, Muzafer, viii, 72n
Single-test system of selecting students,
　　9n, 97n
Sociogram
　　defined, 11
　　constructing, 20–26
　　following up clues of, 26–44
　　leads from interviews and, 34–38
　　limitations of, 34, 90
　　sample form, 25
　　speediest construction of, 21–26
Sociogroup, 92
　　and psychegroup continuum, 91–93
　　collective goals of, 92
Sociometric analysis
　　grade-wide, 57
　　school-wide, 56
Sociometric Analysis Schedule, 31–32
Sociometric choice
　　emphases by age level, 22, 74–78
　　differing potentials in, 98
　　graduated, according to stages of de-
　　　velopment, 88
　　nature of, 72–74
　　See also Psychegroup; Sociogroup
Sociometric continuum of criteria, 91
Sociometric grouping arrangements
　　clubs and Hi-Y organizations, 60–65

Sociometric group arrangements—*Continued*
committees, 18, 48, 58–59, 70
exceptional, 50, 67n
Girl Scouts, 66–70
homeroom, 16
limitations of, 90
playing, 20
seating, 14, 16, 33, 44, 48, 51, 56, 85–86, 91, 92, 93
sororities, 61–66
work projects, 14–16, 18, 20, 58–59, 70, 91ff
See also Principles of sociometric placement
Sociometric position, values linked to, 1, 4, 7
study of, 11, 37, 43–44
Sociometric Tabulation Form, 21
Sociometric test(s)
administration of, 13–19
analyzing results of, 21–34
defined, 11–12
essentials of, 18–19
exceptional placement from, 50, 67n
inhibiting factors avoided in, 14
instructions to young children, 17, 36
importance of timing in, 45, 58
importance of criteria to results of, 45, 90–93, 96
not a test of friendship, 11, 17
selecting situation of, 13–14
series of, needed, 11, 14–15, 44–47
time intervals for retesting, 44–45
word "test" avoided in, 15
wording question of, 15–17, 61
See also Principles of sociometric placement

Sociometric Work Schedule (comparative analyses), 46
Sociometry
defined, 11
distinctive worth of, 13
Stability of choice, 47
first choices, 89

Taba, Hilda, 12, 54
Tally of Sociometric Positions (sample form), 23
Teacher's Home Interview Schedule, 41–43
Teacher's role
in developing choice potential, 78, 90, 96, 98–99
in sociometric arrangement. See Principles of sociometric placement
in sociometric testing, 18–19, 34
Thelen, Herbert A., 98n
Time intervals for retesting. See Sociometric test(s)

Unchosen individuals, 28
home setting related to, 44
task setting related to, 93

Validity, intercultural sociometric, viii
Validity of choices, 71

Weld, Lindsay, 36n
Wilson, M. O., viii, 72n

AMERICAN COUNCIL ON EDUCATION

ARTHUR S. ADAMS, *President*

The American Council on Education is a *council* of national educational associations; organizations having related interests; approved universities, colleges, teachers colleges, junior colleges, technological schools, and selected private secondary schools; state departments of education; city school systems and private school systems; selected educational departments of business and industrial companies; voluntary associations of higher education in the states; and large public libraries. It is a center of cooperation and coordination whose influence has been apparent in the shaping of American educational policies and the formation of educational practices during the past forty-one years.